Jim faced mortality with his cancer and was reminded that only a few things are important to make a life worthy. He has shared them here, and they are a gift. Thank you, Jim.

—**Dr. Henry Cloud,** psychologist;
New York Times bestselling author

A lot of parenting books produce anxiety. They tell you that you're just not measuring up. This is one of the few books that will relieve your fears. Delightful, practical, and at times profound, *Have Serious Fun* gives you a roadmap to a better you and a better family.

—**Carey Nieuwhof,** author, speaker, podcaster

When many of us are bogged down by fear and exhaustion because of the pandemic, social division, and unrest, along with just plain anxiety and uncertainty, Dr. Jim Burns gives us a necessary reminder: have fun. Play. Be silly. Unplug. Be thankful. Focus. "Have serious fun" and the twelve other principles in this book almost feel alien in this time of heightened worry and fear, but this is exactly when we need Jim's message the most.

—**Albert Tate,** pastor, Fellowship Monrovia

After devouring *Have Serious Fun* by my dear friend Jim Burns, I improved my schedule and relationship choices the very next day. Unlike any book I've read recently, this book will immediately shape your most important decisions and set you on a better trajectory in your life, relationships, and faith.

—**Kara Powell,** PhD, chief of leadership formation, Fuller Seminary; executive director, Fuller Youth Institute; coauthor, *Three Big Questions That Change Every Teenager*

All of us struggle with missing out on life for any number of reasons: stresses, relationship problems, losses, and health issues. We become distracted and anxious and obsess on our challenges, and then wonder where our lives went. Yet the Bible teaches us to number our days, because there are a finite number of them. Jim Burns helps show us how to live fully and right now, in a way that will bring joy and meaning, even in the midst of challenges. Highly recommended.

—**John Townsend,** PhD, author, *New York Times* bestselling *Boundaries*; founder, Townsend Institute for Leadership and Counseling

Jim Burns is a gift. Over the years, his upbeat personality, wise counsel, and grounded insights have added incredible value to my personal growth, my marriage to Leslie, and my professional work. That's why I'm thrilled to recommend this power-packed book of legacy lessons. From the first chapter to the last, you'll find ready-made applications to your life, written in Jim's trademark easy-to-read style. Don't miss out on this valuable message.

—**Les Parrott,** PhD, author, *New York Times* #1 bestseller *Saving Your Marriage Before It Starts*

When you spend time with Jim Burns, you quickly realize that he's someone you want to hang out with—a lot. So many of my favorite conversations include Jim around the table, and so much of what I've learned in life comes from his influence. What's made him such a relatable friend shows up quite clearly in these pages. He reminds us that we can take our fun seriously, but that serious can be fun too.

—**Reggie Joiner,** founder/CEO, Orange/reThink

This powerful volume is filled with invaluable insights and advice about living the kind of abundant life Jesus envisions for all of his people.

—Jim Daly, president, Focus on the Family

Have Serious Fun is like the Magna Carta for a life without regrets. Jim's thirteen principles leave us the legacy of an elegant rhythm we can all dance to.

—Dr. Wayne Cordeiro, New Hope Church and College

As a fellow cancer survivor, I read Jim Burns's latest book with great expectancy. It did not disappoint. The book is chock full of essential principles for living life well, along with practical lessons for health, balance, and success.

—Pat Williams, NBA Hall of Fame;
author, *Revolutionary Leadership*

Don't let the title fool you. This book is about so much more than fun. This is perhaps Jim's greatest book because it is jammed full of wisdom that is life changing, especially— for me—the thank therapy chapter. I traveled with Jim and heard him speak on this and it has become part of my mood-elevation program. Get this book and read it to your kids more than once. Jim has serious integrity. He is at the top of my most admired man list. You will not be disappointed in the take-away value of this book.

—Steve Arterburn, national radio host,
New Life Live; bestselling author

Perhaps Jim's best and most important book. Priceless insight, easy to read, super inspiring, deeply thought provoking, and filled with practical ways to experience God's best for your life. I highly recommend it.

—Chip Ingram, founder and CEO, Living on the Edge; author, *Yes! You Really Can Change*

I've heard wisdom defined as "skill in everyday living." By that definition, this book is filled with incredible wisdom. These are important lessons that each one of us needs to learn and relearn throughout our lives. What a great gift from a trusted friend.

—**Bob Lepine,** cohost, *FamilyLife Today*

Have Serious Fun

AND 12 OTHER PRINCIPLES
TO MAKE EACH DAY COUNT

JIM BURNS

ZONDERVAN
BOOKS

ZONDERVAN BOOKS

Have Serious Fun
Copyright © 2021 by Jim Burns

Requests for information should be addressed to:
Zondervan, *3900 Sparks Dr. SE, Grand Rapids, Michigan 49546*

Zondervan titles may be purchased in bulk for educational, business, fundraising, or sales promotional use. For information, please email SpecialMarkets@Zondervan.com.

ISBN 978-0-310-36259-3 (softcover)
ISBN 978-0-310-36261-6 (audio)
ISBN 978-0-310-36260-9 (ebook)

The author is represented by the literary agency of WordServe Literary, Centennial, CO, www.wordserveliterary.com.

Cover design: James W. Hall IV
Cover photos: TriggerPhoto / iStock; Silberkorn / Depositphotos
Author photo: Michelle Kim
Interior design: Sara Colley

Printed in the United States of America

21 22 23 24 25 26 27 28 29 30 31 32 /LSC/ 12 11 10 9 8 7 6 5 4 3 2 1

For my daughters,
Christy Meredith
Rebecca Joy
Heidi Michelle
And the legacy continues.

CONTENTS

FOREWORD

Most of us would like to leave the world a better place than we found it. Most of us would also like to have fun in the process. If these desires resonate with you, this book is for you. When I read the subtitle, *And Twelve Other Principles to Make Each Day Count*, I knew that this book would be practical and that it would address real-life issues. I was not disappointed. Each chapter helped me reflect on my life and ask, "What can I learn from this chapter that will make me a better person?"

I have known Jim Burns for many years. He has invested his life in counseling, speaking, and writing about how to have good relationships. I have always admired the practicality of his writing. In many ways, *Have Serious Fun* is a legacy book for Jim. When the cancer diagnosis came, Jim accepted the reality that none of us wants to think about, but which all of us must face: death is a part of life. He stared death in the face and then survived, hopefully for many more years. Anyone who has had the unwelcome guest of a disease that often leads to death can identify with the sobering effect it has on one's perspective. Things that once seemed important fade in significance, and we focus on the things that are really important. We want to make each day count, and we still want to have fun. This book will help you accomplish this goal—without the trauma of a life-threatening disease.

Our lives are never static. We are either growing or regressing. We never stand still. The older I get, the more I reflect on the legacy I am leaving for those who come after me. I have often been sobered by the questions: What if my children turn out to be like me? What if they eventually have a marriage like mine? Along the journey, these questions have helped me make constructive changes in the way I live.

This book is not preachy. It is the overflow of a life well lived. Jim shares his failures and course corrections, both before and after being visited by cancer. I found every chapter to be thoughtful and challenging. If you want to have serious fun and make each day count, you have chosen the right book.

—Gary Chapman, author of
The Five Love Languages

PREFACE

*You can't go back and change the
beginning, but you can start where
you are and change the ending.*

—C. S. Lewis

Several years ago, my doctor called and asked
me to come to his office that afternoon. He said,
"Also, bring your wife." When I heard those words, I
assumed the news wasn't great. It wasn't. He told us
I had cancer. I ended up having surgery at one of the
finest cancer-treatment hospitals in the world, City
of Hope in Los Angeles. To be honest, I never thought
I was going to die.[1] This may sound crazy, but I was
dealing with several issues in our family and ministry,
and hearing that I had cancer was just one more item
to add to my list of things to do. I know . . . I probably
needed counseling because of the way I handled it. I
even went so far as to ask my surgeon if it was possible

to postpone my surgery a few months so I could finish my busy speaking season. Like I said, I probably needed counseling.

The night before my surgery, Cathy and I stayed at a hotel near the hospital. Though I'd never prayed this prayer as a kid, I found myself thinking the words of what I had always considered to be a morbid kids' prayer: "If I should die before I wake, I pray the Lord my soul to take." It's kind of surprising what you think and pray about as you face death or at least major cancer surgery. Strangely enough, I was at peace with my eventual death. I believe in eternity. I wasn't praying out of fear, but rather I was thinking about legacy, which became important to me through my bout with cancer. Even that night, I kept asking myself, "What are the lessons and principles most important to me that I want to pass on to my children?" In the middle of the night, I got out of bed and wrote in my journal many of the lessons in this book. I titled the page of these scribbled principles "Life-Transforming Thoughts for Relationships, Leadership, and Personal Life."

The surgery was successful and I'm still cancer free, and I've added a few more lessons since that night. I hadn't planned to write a book from those pages. I'd simply wanted to pass the thoughts on to my children and grandchildren. A friend, knowing I had written them down, asked me to speak at a conference where he was gathering some key leaders from around the United States. My typical speaking topics include marriage, parenting, and family issues, but he asked me to speak on "Life-Changing Lessons on Relationships, Leadership, and Personal Life" and then to remain onstage to take questions from the crowd. When the day arrived to speak to this incredible group of leaders, I wondered whether I had anything to say that could possibly be life-changing for them. After all, these were just my thoughts and experiences, and I'd done little research. I spoke for exactly forty-two minutes, anticipating only a few questions. An hour later, the questions, reactions, and comments were still going strong and we were forced to end the session so the next one could begin.

What I realized that day was that I had somehow struck a nerve in many of those people. My issues were their issues, my struggles were their struggles, my hopes were their hopes. And I learned that my answers were what they were looking for. People started asking me to speak on the subject of this book. Today, hardly a week goes by when I don't speak, do an interview, or have a personal conversation with someone about one or more of these lessons. Who would have thought that scribbling a few words in my journal, after saying a goofy prayer, would not only change my life but give others hope for their journey?

I recently participated in a webinar with leaders from around the world. The emcee asked me what I had been doing during this time of Covid and sheltering in place. He knew that I usually speak about a hundred times a year and that I wasn't exactly doing that now. I told him I was having a great time writing a book on thirteen life-changing lessons that I discovered as I faced my mortality because of cancer. He smiled and said, "Oh, it's your legacy book!" At first, I wanted to say, "No, absolutely not." Instead, I quoted a classic comedy movie with a cultlike following. In *Monty Python and the Holy Grail*, a sick man is brought out by his family to be picked up with others who had died of a plague. He looks up at them and says, "I'm not dead yet!" They laughed, but the more time I put into writing this book, the more I realized I *was* writing a legacy book. It's very personal. My goal is to open up my life to you and share the vital lessons for a good life that I have learned and want to apply so my family will catch them before I'm gone. I believe it's one of the most important things I've ever written, and I trust it will help you too. I'm always open if you'd like to drop me a line to let me know how you've been affected by what I've tried to capture here.

Thank you for reading and for continuing to believe we can make a difference in the lives of people around us, especially the kids.

—Jim Burns, Dana Point,
California (info@HomeWord.com)

P.S. By the way, I've found that many people learn best not when *I* talk but when *they* talk and exchange ideas. If you'd like to discuss these thirteen lessons in your small group, a great companion course is available on my website: HomeWord.com.

THANK YOU

- Cathy: I'm so glad you said yes! And have continued to say yes.
- Christy, Rebecca, Heidi, Steve, Matt, James, Charlotte, Huxley: You are the reason I wrote this book (Ps. 100:5).
- Cindy Ward: Your partnership in our mission at HomeWord brings great joy to so many. Especially me.
- Rod Emery, Randy Bramel, Tom Purcell, Terry Hartshorn: I can't think of a better way to have spent Tuesday mornings the last eighteen years of my life. Your wisdom, generosity, and friendship are always inspiring.
- Carol Zinngrabe: The filming of *Have Serious Fun*, as well as so many life-changing projects, is all because of your and Bob's generous and beautiful hearts.

- Todd Dean, Doug Fields, Shawn King, Doug Webster: What a joy it is to work and dream together about helping families succeed.
- Greg Johnson: There is not a better literary agent in the world.
- Mick Silva: How did I get so fortunate to have you lead the editing process? You are the best. It is a joy to work with you and the team at HarperCollins/Zondervan.

Lesson 1

HAVE SERIOUS FUN

*If you are not having fun, you're
doing something wrong.*

—GROUCHO MARX

I can truthfully say that I have never enjoyed sitting at the kitchen table paying bills. Even if I have the money to pay the bills, and there have been times when I didn't, just the effort of doing that chore is never on my list of things that make me happy. Okay, I know I have a PhD, but I was never a numbers whiz, and today I probably wouldn't do well in sixth-grade math.

One evening, Cathy (my amazing wife, whom you will get to know better in this book) and I were paying the bills. It wasn't how I'd wanted to spend our evening together. Our youngest daughter, Heidi, came bouncing into the kitchen bursting with energy. She had just finished babysitting for our good friends Scott and Anita. She announced, "Scott and Anita are the best parents I have ever known! Their kids are great! Their dog is great! They are so fun and funny. I just love them."

I'm not usually all that defensive, but I looked up from paying the bills, thinking, "If Scott and Anita are so great, what do you think of us?" Another lesson I should have put in this book: "Don't say everything you think." Instead, I smiled and said, "You are so right, and they're some of my favorite people too! Did you know Mom and I have known them since they were in high school?"

She looked puzzled. "Yeah, they told me. They said you were their youth pastors. You know what else they said? They said you were both so fun and funny." It was a statement, but she asked it more as a question: "So what happened to you?"

The next day, I happened to be at our local pharmacy. For some reason, I found myself staring at a shelf of refrigerator magnets. I saw the perfect one, so I bought my first and only refrigerator magnet ever. It read, "Are we having fun yet?"

After my cancer scare, I didn't decide immediately to work on my 401(k) or design a plan for world peace or find a better software program to pay the bills. But I did write in my journal these three words: "Have serious fun!" They became a major lesson and goal for the rest of my life. This may sound like an oversimplification, but a family that doesn't play well together probably isn't doing all that well. Fun, play, humor, and the building of lifelong traditions are all essential traits of a healthy person and a healthy family. Even an enjoyable work environment is a heck of a lot better than a stressful, hectic, boring, mundane, tedious, miserable, or mind-numbing atmosphere.

You really can't do much about how others do life, but *you* can choose to have serious fun. It's a choice you make every day. It doesn't have to be giddy, extroverted, party-animal fun, but a playful attitude just might be the missing ingredient to a more meaningful life.

You might ask, "What about all the negative circumstances of my life?" I know it's complicated, but even amid difficult circumstances, it's still possible to choose fun.

Since my cancer surgery, I have found that one of the most important ingredients to a successful life is the choice to have serious fun. One of my goals for this year is "more play, less work." How about you? I'm not necessarily succeeding 24/7, but it has helped improve my perspective tremendously. And I can say with certainty that the more I practice it, the better I get at remembering it the next time.

How's the fun factor in your life? If you are like

most of us, the stress of simply doing life sometimes clouds the joy that comes from having fun. Here is a good proverb to remember: "A cheerful heart is good medicine, but a crushed spirit dries up the bones" (Prov. 17:22). Another version says it this way: "A cheerful heart is good medicine, but a broken spirit saps a person's strength" (NLT). Obviously, life throws a lot of tough stuff at us that can bring pain and sorrow, but even a little bit of fun can keep our strength from being sapped.

Dr. Norman Cousins developed a life-threatening disease of the connective tissue called degenerative collagen illness. He was hospitalized with severe pain, high fever, and almost complete paralysis of the legs, neck, and back. Dr. Cousins beat the odds of 500 to 1 and recovered. In his classic book, *Anatomy of an Illness*, he chronicled the story of his recovery. Cousins believed that laughter and positive emotions could help his healing significantly. With his doctor's consent, he checked himself out of the hospital and into a nice hotel across the street. At the hotel, he focused on a continuous stream of humorous films and other types of laughing matter. He later claimed that ten minutes of belly-rippling laughter gave him two hours of pain-free sleep that not even morphine had provided him. His condition steadily improved, and within six months, he was back on his feet.

Dr. Cousins, who taught at UCLA in the department

of psychiatry and biobehavioral sciences, never claimed laughter and fun can take away all your problems, but throughout his career, he helped change the mindset of the medical world on the importance of fun and how it can be a determining factor in healing.

Play, the Missing Ingredient

Many experts tell us that the family that prays together stays together. I believe that. But I also believe that the family that *plays* together stays together. Although we weren't the worst family at having fun, we had become quite intense and serious. We had allowed stress to rob some of the joy of our family life. This doesn't mean that you should ignore your problems. We need to feel our feelings and process them, and sometimes that is best done with a counselor, pastor, or friend. But play had become the missing ingredient in my marriage, parenting, and work. After the cancer diagnosis, I found that play and serious fun became the glue our family needed to draw closer together. Play opens closed spirits and can even heal broken relationships. I had to learn that sometimes words don't lead to connection with a loved one, but connection through fun leads to more words. I love what author Leonard Sweet said many years ago about marriage: "For a marriage to sing and dance, for two people to make beautiful music together, they need to play, not work, at their marriage."[2]

Naturally there is work involved in making a marriage strong or bringing a family together, but if you want your family and personal life to really thrive, you can't forget to ask yourself, "Are we having fun yet?" If your fun quotient is already met, congratulations! This is an affirmation of your good work at having fun. If your fun quotient needs some help, then the good news is you can do something about it as you move toward positive change. Here's what I have learned as I lean into choosing to have serious fun.

Play Builds Great Memories

Have you ever noticed that some of the best conversation is often about positive family experiences at extended family gatherings? It was the time Grandpa fell into the lake while fishing or the time the entire family went to Disneyland and rode the same ride three times. Many of those conversations center around the good and fun memories of meaningful experiences. We tend to remember the vibe, the laughter, and the togetherness. We also remember the harder times, but it's usually the fun times that bring smiles to our faces. I'm not a person who has many regrets, and I don't hyper focus on the few regrets I do have. But after my surgery, I wrote in my journal, "If I had my life to do over again, I would order up less stress and have more fun. I would be more proactive about vacations and play and laughter and connection." It's smart to build fun traditions for you and your family. The key word is proactive. You can be more intentional at having fun. Do whatever it takes. Stay away from the twenty-four-hour negative newsfeed, take a vacation, a walk, a break. Add a new skill to your repertoire like photography or painting or singing or tennis. Connect with old friends and make new ones. Fun will fill your memory bank and give you joy.

Play Reduces Stress

As I focused on having serious fun, I remembered my PhD research on the traits of a healthy family. One of those traits is playing together. Play brings families together, while building more affirmation and support. Families who have focused fun times together have a greater sense of belonging and joy as a family unit. Another interesting fact is that most people also have lower stress no matter what their circumstances. How's the tension in your life right now? Some stress in your life is not bad, especially if it's short lived. But constantly feeling out of control and overstressed can be the root of broken relationships and health risks.

Here are just a few ways to know whether you are overstressed:

- Do you experience a sense of urgency and hurry or have no time to release, play, or relax?
- Do you have underlying tension that causes sharp words, harsh startups to conversations, hurt feelings, or misunderstood messages?
- Are you preoccupied with escaping, finding peace, going on vacation, quitting work, or dreaming of a life with less stress?
- Do you constantly feel frustration about getting things done that you can't shut off?
- Do you have a nagging desire to find a simpler life?

None of these factors is necessarily unhealthy in and of itself, but when they are added together and you experience them for an extended period, it is definitely time to take a break. Maybe an eight-day, do-nothing-but-play vacation to find perspective is what you need. How crazy are we to raise our blood pressure to dangerous heights and work our fingers to the bone, to be overcommitted and fatigued most days, and then try to recuperate with a day off when we are still connected to our cell phones, computers, and iPads 24/7? Then we go right back to the grind. Most of us know deep down in our hearts that something is terribly wrong with our lifestyle choices if we are constantly under stress.

Recently, Cathy and I sensed we had reached our max. We'd had some stressful challenges at work, a couple of adult kids had boomeranged home to live with us, and our world had turned upside down with COVID-19, protests, and a divided nation. We decided to just stop it all. Someone once told us, "Life is too short not to go on a spontaneous road trip." We got in the car and drove up the California coast to the beautiful little town of Cambria.

We love it there, our first visit now forty-six years ago on our honeymoon. The stores were still closed because of COVID-19 and only a few restaurants were serving takeout, but that didn't matter. It was time for a break and some fun. We took extra-long walks at Moonstone Beach, and there was an afternoon nap or two. We didn't need to take 140 photos of the sunset, but that's what we did. We laughed. We focused on each other and rekindled romance. Some intentional serious fun caused us to have much clearer communication. We disciplined ourselves to stay away from the negative newsfeed. We knew it wouldn't go away, but for that short time, we were determined to refresh our souls.

As we were driving back home, we agreed we needed to commit to having more serious fun. The problems of our world hadn't disappeared, but that time to play gave us the energy and courage to step back into the not-so-fun moments of life.

How about you? What would it take for you to be more intentional about having serious fun? Each person is different and each situation in life is a bit unique, so what can *you* do today to create some serious fun in your life? In the words of Charles Spurgeon, "It is not how much we have but how much we enjoy that makes happiness."

For busy people, fun takes work and intentionality. What do you need to let go of to make some happiness in your life this week, this month?

Lesson 2

ATTITUDE IS EVERYTHING

Some cause happiness wherever
they go; others whenever they go.
—OSCAR WILDE

During a difficult season in my life, I asked a mentor of mine if we could have lunch. He had always given me such great advice and perspective. This time he listened, didn't say much, and then wrote a few Bible verses on a napkin and handed it to me before we left the restaurant. Don't get me wrong, I love the wisdom of the Bible, but to be honest, I was looking for more. I stuffed the napkin in my pocket, and that night my wife asked about our lunch. I told her I was a tad bit disappointed by his lack of advice. I told her that he had simply written a couple of Bible verses on a napkin. She asked what they were, and I had to admit I hadn't bothered to look at them. So I pulled the napkin out of my pocket and read what he wrote: "Rejoice always, pray continually, give thanks in all circumstances; for this is God's will for you in Christ Jesus" (1 Thess. 5:16–18). Those verses ended up becoming part of a major life message for me and helped me through times of struggle and conflict and my cancer scare. I'm not exaggerating when I say that they changed my life, because they helped change my attitude. Let me explain.

Cultivate Joy

As I investigated the Scripture passage my friend John wrote on the napkin and how it relates to my attitude, I wrote at the top of a page in my journal the word joy. Then I wrote, "My goal is joy!"

"Rejoice Always"

"Rejoice always." Another more modern translation of that verse reads, "Be full of joy." I then circled the word joy. I knew from past study that when a person has deep-rooted joy, it is something much more than happiness after eating a great meal or watching a wonderful movie. Joy comes from the inside, and it's connected to the well-being of the soul. Part of my journey toward deeper joy is knowing it's a choice and not usually based on circumstance or chance.

About that time, I was having dinner with my friend Henry Cloud. Over the years, Henry has been one of the leading voices on the subject of creating healthy relational boundaries and finding joy in the midst of difficult circumstances. At dinner that night, he gave me a great illustration about developing joy. He said, "Yes, you can make joy a goal and choice for your life, but you can't just will to have joy. You have to choose the practices and activities that enrich your life with joy, just like you would cultivate a garden." Hmm, a lot like deciding to have serious fun and then implementing a plan to do so.

Here is another insight I learned around that time: circumstances are not as important to our joy as most of us would think. Two people can have a similar negative circumstance, and one of those people can rise above it and still have joy, while the other doesn't. It's more a matter of mindset than circumstance. I saw a poster recently in a hospital waiting room that read, "Life isn't about waiting for the storm to pass . . . it's about learning to dance in the rain" (Vivian Greene). Many years ago, a scientific researcher named Sonja Lyubomirsky wrote a book called *The How of Happiness*. In this book, she developed a simple "Pie Chart of Happiness."

Pie Chart of Happiness

What Determines Happiness?

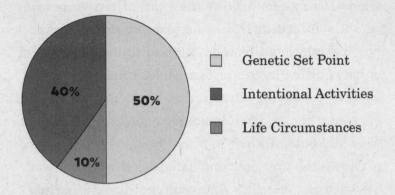

Whether or not this is accurate in your life, the pie chart reminds us that there are at least three major influences to develop deeper joy: genetics, circumstances, and activities. The research also reveals that our circumstances have the least to do with it. If only 10 percent of our joy or happiness comes from circumstances, and there is not much we can do about our genetics or biological set point (50 percent), then our focus needs to be on activities and choices we make that increase our happiness. While there's still the matter of deciding whether a brisk walk or another Twinkie will garner the results we seek, when you think about it, having such control over our attitudes is good news. Back to what Henry Cloud told me at dinner that night, that our joy mainly comes from our activities and life practices: this translates to our attitude.

While battling cancer, I realized that it really had been a draining season of life and that the joy that I'd had glimpses of at times seemed out of reach. As I studied the word joy in the Bible, I realized that more than five hundred times we are commanded to practice choosing joy above anything else. So almost every morning before I get out of bed, I recite Psalm 118:24: "This is the day the LORD has made; let us rejoice and be glad in it" (NIV 1984). Repeating that verse day after day reminds me that he is God and I am not, and that my joy comes from healthy practices and activities. It's a daily practice, more of a running stream than a stagnant pool. Here's the bottom line: You won't get joy from others or from money or from fame. Joy is an inside job, and you make it happen.

"Pray Continually"

If my goal was to have a deep-seated mindset of joy, how could I attain it? The words "pray continually" didn't seem to help, but as I investigated what Scripture says about prayer, I realized there is an intriguing promise connected to it. "Do not be anxious about anything, but in every situation, by prayer and petition, with thanksgiving, present your requests to God. And the peace of God, which transcends all understanding, will guard your hearts and your minds in Christ Jesus" (Phil. 4:6–7). The more I looked at this, the more I wondered, "If I spend time regularly with God in prayer,

just talking with him about everything, with thanksgiving, will I experience more peace?" All I'd studied
and witnessed about people who live with joy seemed
to indicate this was the "secret sauce" for being more
at peace. Even more interesting was that most of them
had the same relational and work problems anyone else
has, but they didn't get as bent out of shape about them.
They had already chosen a different mindset.

So I decided to commit to twenty minutes of prayer
a day. To some people, that might sound super spiritual; to others, it might seem spiritually wimpy. But
over the long haul, spending twenty minutes a day
reading Scriptures like these, praying and journaling
my thoughts, and looking for any gratitude I could find
grounded me in my situations and often changed my
perspective. It's no magic formula. There are times I
don't remember what I've read or prayed about. (But
then, I don't always remember what I ate for dinner
a week ago, but somehow it still nourished me then.)
And there are times when I read, pray, and journal
and, instead of peace, the result is focusing all day on a
fear or worry. But I can say with confidence that most
days, this twenty-minute discipline has worked for me.

Let the reader beware: results may vary! One day I
was talking with leadership expert and author Nancy
Ortberg about spiritual disciplines and joy. I told her
that I read through the One Year Bible every year, and
I pray and journal. She smiled and said, "That's what

my husband, John, does. I think that is sooo boring!"
She said she needed to walk in nature and listen to God
instead. Obviously, she recognized the need for prayer,
and she wasn't opposed to the discipline I was talking
about, but my routine just didn't work for her. When it
comes to prayer and cultivating a joyful attitude, there
just isn't a one-size-fits-all regimen. Do what works for
you. I'm typically not a person who finds cutesy little
formulas from the Bible helpful. But the Scripture
my friend John handed to me on the napkin that day
translated into "joy = giving thanks in prayer."

And that has stuck with me and done some good
work on my crusty soul.

"Give Thanks in All Circumstances"

This is the phrase I had the most trouble with,
but eventually it became the most powerful one of all.
In all circumstances? Really? Was I truly supposed
to thank God for the death of a parent or for war or
for a friend's drug addiction? Then I noticed it didn't
say give thanks *for it*; it said *in it*. Well, that made
all the difference in the world! I could thank God *in*
my mother's passing, even though I grieved her loss.
Her passing freed her from the pain of her cancer. She
was with God in heaven. There were plenty of things I
could thank God for *in* my circumstances, once I slowed
down enough to consider everything. Thanksgiving
truly is a key that can help even in your unhappiest

and most depressed moments. I'm now convinced that a discipline of thankfulness is tied to our attitude in any circumstance.

Here is what I think: Thankfulness transcends circumstances. Your circumstances may stink and rightly cause you to want to throw a fit, but seeking the things you're still grateful for can keep your head above your attitude, and that makes all the difference in the world. I learned that my circumstance may never change, but my attitude can change how I view it.

Perhaps you've seen the kitchen sign that reads, "I complained because I had no shoes until I met a man who had no feet." I like what Martin Luther once said: "I cannot stop the birds from flying over my head, but I can stop them from building nests in my hair." Shift your perspective. Who doesn't want to be a thankful, grateful person in all things? This is what has changed my attitude about life the most.

A few years ago, I interviewed Joni Eareckson Tada. Joni has spent her entire adult life confined to a wheelchair. As I prepared for the interview with her, I knew that as radiant as she is, she has faced extreme pain and suffering. Her inspiring story is one of my favorites of all time. As she wheeled herself into our studio, I was once again overcome by her joyful and radiant spirit, despite all of her challenges. I put all my notes aside, looked her in the eyes, and asked,

"Joni, how do you remain so joyful in the midst of all your physical struggles?" She paused for an extra-long time. Silence is never comfortable for radio. Finally, she said, "Jim, I think I just disciplined myself for so many years to give thanks in all circumstances that it has become my reflex reaction."

Tears came to my eyes as I looked at this beautiful woman who has been confined in a chair for all her adult life. Joni ignited in me a desire for a new way to live, the key to a joy-filled life: to discipline myself to make an attitude of thanksgiving prayer my reflex reaction.

Anne Lamott once wrote, "You breathe in gratitude, and you breathe it out, too."[3] Dallas Willard died May 8, 2013. He was truly one of the greatest thinkers, writers, and philosophers of the century. Lying in his hospital bed, about to leave this world at any moment, all of a sudden he leaned his head back slightly as if looking toward heaven, and with his eyes closed, he smiled and in a voice clearer than he'd had in many days said, "Thank you." Soon after that, he entered eternity with the one to whom he had given thanks. What a life of cultivating a joyful attitude. These are people who cultivated a right attitude in the midst of tough circumstances. If they can do it, so can you and I.

Seems like a worthy enough idea to practice, don't you agree?

Lesson 3

PRACTICE THANK
THERAPY

I would maintain that thanks
are the highest form of thought;
and that gratitude is happiness
doubled by wonder.

—G. K. CHESTERTON

I've run only one marathon in my life. I came in 4,456th. Obviously I wasn't a front-runner. As I shuffled across the finish line, I greeted my wife and kids by saying, "I never want to do this again!" And I haven't. On the other hand, one of the true heroes of my life was a twenty-two-year-old marathon runner named Terry Fox. Terry was only eighteen years old when he learned he had osteosarcoma (bone cancer). His right leg was amputated six inches above his knee. While in the hospital, he was so overcome by the suffering of other cancer patients, he decided to run the entire length of Canada to raise money for cancer research, to help others. He called his journey the Marathon of Hope. I remember watching news clips of this young man with a prosthetic leg, in the middle of nowhere, running always with pain. I remember a moment when he was in the middle of what looked like a cornfield somewhere in one of Canada's Atlantic provinces. By this time, he had already covered 4,500 kilometers, running the distance of a marathon every day. A television interviewer asked him, "Terry, how are you feeling today?" Terry smiled and said, "I'm tired. I ran forty-two kilometers [twenty-six miles] today." The camera focused on his prosthetic leg. The interviewer asked, "Do you think you can make it all the way across Canada?" Again, he smiled and said something so profound I will never forget it. "I'm thankful for every breath. I'm glad God gave me today, and I'm going to live one day at a time."

It wasn't long after that statement that the cancer appeared with a vengeance in Terry's lungs. He was forced to stop running. The world was stunned and saddened when Terry passed away the next year. This heroic Canadian was gone, but his legacy has continued with more than $750 million having been raised worldwide in his name for cancer research.

The legacy Terry left for me was that a young man of twenty-two years could say, "I'm thankful for every breath." He acknowledged that God gave him each day, and he focused on living one day at a time. I'm not sure whether Terry knew he was quoting Jesus when he said that. Here is what Jesus said in his Sermon on the Mount: "So don't be anxious about tomorrow. God will take care of your tomorrow too. Live one day at a time" (Matt. 6:34 TLB).

Thank Therapy

Terry Fox practiced thank therapy. He didn't know or use the term, but there is no doubt in my mind that thank therapy is what helped him break through the barriers in his life. One of his many quotable quotes is, "I got satisfaction out of doing things that were difficult. It was an incredible feeling. The pain was there, but the pain didn't matter."[4] There is no doubt that practicing thank therapy has changed my life. When people ask me what lesson in this book has helped me the most, I tell them it's to practice thank therapy.

Thank therapy is daily acknowledging God's gift of life, while living one day at a time, and being thankful. This Bible verse summarizes this truth for me: "Devote yourselves to prayer, being watchful and thankful" (Col. 4:2). As I've said, the discipline of spending time in prayer every day was a game-changer for me. Being mindful of God or being thankful does not come naturally for me. So each day, I write down in my journal at least twenty reasons why I'm thankful. Before you get too impressed by the magic number of twenty, most days the reasons look similar: the names of my wife, children, and grandchildren make the list almost every day. It usually doesn't take me longer than a minute or two. It's the *habit* of acknowledging those reasons that makes all the difference in the world. I've challenged thousands of people to practice thank therapy, and I've never had one person try it and come back telling me it wasn't worth their time and energy. Thankfulness transcends our circumstances and gives us a better perspective.

I'd be making a mistake if I didn't challenge you to stop reading right now for five minutes to take your first dose of thank therapy. Even this morning I wrote down more than twenty reasons to be thankful. If you looked at the list, you wouldn't find anything surprising. It was mainly about my family, my health, beautiful California weather, HomeWord being a great place to work, the chance to spend time writing today, and other basic things. I even wrote down a few challenges that I'm thankful for that are helping me to be a better person. As I reflect, my morning thank-therapy exercise simply reminds me of all that I have to be grateful for. There are plenty of challenges in life, but I can either put off thinking about them for the moment or be thankful amid those challenges. Some of the greatest challenges in my life have been the greatest gifts for refining me. And I know if I'm patient, my challenges can become my biggest points of gratefulness too.

Make Thankfulness a Habit

Everyone has some good habits and some not-so-good habits. Experts tell us it takes three weeks to form a habit and another three weeks to solidify it for a lifetime. What if you practiced thank therapy every day for three weeks? And then did it again for another three weeks? If you practiced thank therapy five minutes a day for forty-two days, you would spend only 210 minutes in the next six weeks creating a life-changing habit that will benefit you on several levels for the rest of your life. That's an investment of only 3.5 hours to make you a better, wiser, happier person focused on the right and good things of your life. That's giving up a couple of TV episodes of *Friends* or *NCIS* or, for me, *Hawaii Five-0*. Another way to look at it is it's five minutes less time on social media. (You probably need to reduce your social media time anyway!)

Cathy and I had just finished a wonderful week speaking at a conference center in the Santa Cruz

Mountains in Northern California. We had a great time. Then we spent a night in Carmel, one of our favorite towns along the coast. It was a special time of doing what we love to do: walking the beach, exploring the town, eating Italian with cannoli for dessert, and of course, sharing some great romance. (I'm blushing.)

The next day after a lazy breakfast, we hopped in the car and started driving down the coast on Highway 1. In my mind, it just doesn't get better than this. As we were heading out of Carmel, Cathy bluntly said, "I think you are getting a double chin!" Then she playfully grabbed the flap that was apparently hanging below my chin. My reaction was anger. And when I get angry, I usually don't yell on the outside but scream on the inside and crawl into my "Jim cave." That's what I did. I was fuming and thinking, "How could she say something so mean and hurtful to me after such a great week? What is wrong with her?"

She, on the other hand, was enjoying the drive along the coast, even pointing out dramatic cliff views and thinking she saw a dolphin or two along the way.

After I'd been driving about forty-five minutes in sulking silence, it hit me. That morning I had practiced thank therapy and Cathy had been behind several reasons for my gratitude. It was as if I heard a still, small voice in my head saying, "Practice your new habit of thank therapy!" So I said to myself, with gritted teeth, "Thank you for Cathy, even if she made a very crummy comment."

Then I softened a bit. I thought of everything on my list, being thankful for her fidelity, for her being the incredible mother she is to our children, for her unselfish attitude, for her love for God, and for her authenticity. The list went on and on, perhaps thirty reasons for gratitude. Somewhere between being thankful for her sacrificial love and for her being a wonderful role model, it dawned on me that her comment was not meant to be harmful. I still didn't think her timing was all that perfect, but she intended no malice. I looked over at her and simply said, "Hey, Cathy, I love you, and it was a great week. Thank you!"

She looked back a little surprised and said, "Oh, I thought you were mad at me for telling you I thought you had a double chin!"

I smiled, gave her a kiss on the cheek, and said, "Your timing could have been better, and I'm not even sure I agree, but yes, I am so grateful we are doing this life together."

The Benefits of Gratitude

Here is a bit of science: gratitude is one of the most important ingredients of happiness. In recent years, researchers have begun studying the effects of an attitude of gratitude, and the results are remarkable. Study after study reveals that people who can be grateful for their lives as opposed to grumbling and complaining are healthier, happier, less depressed, and more fulfilled, and have better relationships and many other positive outcomes.

Two Indiana University professors, Joel Wong, associate professor of counseling psychology, and Joshua Brown, professor of psychological brain sciences, did a fascinating research project on people who practice gratitude. Their study yielded several observations, but the two most intriguing are (1) gratitude unshackles us from toxic emotions, and (2) gratitude has lasting healthy effects on the brain. Their summary was that developing gratefulness in our lives (practicing thank therapy) changes us and our brains for the better.[5]

It's a scientific fact that being thankful regardless of your feelings means you can have joy, regardless of your circumstances. Henry Cloud once said, "Our brains and our bodies are wired to respond, to come alive, and to do better when we are practicing certain activities. When we give thanks, our chemistry changes in a positive way."[6]

After my cancer surgery, I began to think much more about people I was deeply grateful to for their influence on my life. I decided to write gratitude letters to as many of these people as I could think of who were still alive. My one regret was that both of my parents had died before I could write them gratitude letters. I wrote to mentors, friends, family, and others who had made a difference in my life. I sensed my brain was being rewired to be grateful instead of complaining and grumbling. If you are anything like I was after my surgery, the writing of a gratitude letter is not only a blessing to the person receiving it but also a wonderful encouragement to you. To quote that great work of philosophy *Winnie-the-Pooh*, "Piglet noticed that even though he had a very small heart, it could hold a rather large amount of gratitude." My friend John Ortberg said it this way: "Gratitude is the ability to experience life as a gift. It liberates us from the prison of self-preoccupation."[7]

Being Thankful Is the Password into God's Presence

There is a spiritual component to thankfulness as well. Two of the greatest themes in the Bible are trust and thankfulness. Being thankful to God and others gives us the right perspective on putting our trust in God, the sustainer and creator of our lives. It's impossible to praise or thank God too much. The psalmist presents an incredible word picture in Psalm 22:3: God inhabits the praise of his people. Another way of putting it is that he is enthroned on the praise of his people. Apparently, thanksgiving with praise is the royal road to draw near to God. When we give God our gratitude, we acknowledge his presence in our lives, and it's much easier to put our trust in him. Thankfulness lifts us above our circumstances, and trust is the channel to give us greater peace and direction. The first Scripture verses my four-year-old grandson learned are Proverbs 3:5–6 (NKJV):

> Trust in the LORD with all your heart,
> And lean not on your own understanding;
> In all your ways acknowledge Him,
> And He shall direct your paths.

God tends to do his greatest works through people with grateful, trusting hearts. Thankfulness opens the door to God's presence. You practice his presence by practicing the discipline of thankfulness.

I met Elaine Robertson when I was in graduate school in Princeton, New Jersey. She was undoubtedly one of the most radiant, thankful people I have ever met. Life was hard for her. She was confined to a wheelchair and suffered from cerebral palsy. Not an easy life. She always intrigued me because of her thankful attitude and joy-filled spirit. One day years after I had graduated and moved away, I was back at Princeton speaking. There she was in the library, just as radiant as ever, even though the years had been rough on her health and body. I invited her to go with me and a few students on a walk around the picturesque Princeton University campus.

As I was wheeling her through the campus toward the beautiful chapel, I whispered in her ear, "Elaine, life's been tough for you, hasn't it? How do you manage to be so beautiful and have such a wonderful attitude in the midst of your obstacles?"

She said, "Jim, stop the wheelchair. I want to sing a song for you."

Okay, it was a little awkward, but I stopped pushing her and faced her. This is the little chorus she sang:

> Jesus, I love you
> I give you my heart
> I live for and thank you daily
> Each day a new start

That was it. Simple. Not even on key. She told Jesus she loved him. She offered her heart and trust to God. She thanked him, and then she did it again the next day and the next. I stood there with tears rolling down my face because we had connected and her words reminded me that in this complicated world, we sometimes miss the beautiful simplicity of cultivating a grateful heart.

Don't miss it: Whatever you're going through, feel it and don't dismiss it. But don't miss out on the blessing of thankfulness in the midst of it. That simple practice can change your life. It has changed mine.

Lesson 4

IF THE DEVIL CAN'T MAKE YOU BAD, HE'LL MAKE YOU BUSY

Fatigue makes cowards of us all.
—VINCE LOMBARDI

Sometimes I refer to times in my life as BC, which stands for "before cancer," or AC, "after cancer."

BC, I ran my life at a very fast pace. I'm not sure I took enough time to smell the roses. Come to think of it, I'm still not sure what roses smell like. AC, I became aware that I needed to "ruthlessly eliminate hurry" from my life. I didn't come up with that phrase. A lot of people much smarter than me have used it.

Perhaps one of the greatest problems in this world is the breathless pace at which we live our lives. Hurry is often the enemy of healthy relationships. Hurry is the enemy of deepening our spiritual lives, and it gets in the way of making good decisions. Hurry and busyness creep up on us and squeeze the joy from our lives. We are far too busy.

I still remember the day I opened a card from my good friend David after graduate school. Cathy and I had decided not to stay for the graduation celebration in order to get a head start driving from Princeton, New Jersey, back to Orange, California, where we were going to work and live. We knew we would miss our time in Princeton, but we were anxious to get on with life and return to our home sweet home. A week after we arrived in California after driving across the country with everything we owned (which wasn't much), I received a nice card from my friend David. We had become great friends in grad school. David wrote, "Jim, we missed you at the graduation ceremony. Just ran across this quote, 'If the devil can't make you bad, he will make you busy.'" He added, "Stay in touch."

Little did David realize how prophetic that phrase was for my life. All these years later, I'm not one to break a marriage vow or embezzle money or not pay taxes, but I can easily fall into the trap of being too busy.

Busyness and hurry are the enemies of a meaningful

life. There might have been a time when I would have equated busyness with success. Not any longer. I often find that busy people are broken people. John Mark Comer says it this way: "Hurry is a form of violence on the soul."[8] There is a huge gap between looking at busyness as success and looking at it as sickness.

Our family really likes hot tubs. There is just something about sitting together in a spa, feeling the warmth of the jets against our backs and engaging in great conversation that draws us together. (I know, talk about a pampered life!) One day we were staying at a friend's condo in Palm Desert, California. Right out back they have a great spa. It was the first day of our vacation, and after dinner we all were going to get in the spa to have some serious fun and connect.

Being the only male in the family, I have no idea why this happens, but I was ready to jump into the spa before anyone else. I switched on the jets and got in. Ahhh, the incredible feeling of the brisk winter air while sitting in a hot tub and staring out at the moon and desert stars. Then right before the rest of the family showed up, the timer for the jets in the spa turned off. I suddenly realized I was sitting in a spa that was in dire need of being cleaned. Dirt and leaves swirled and came to rest as a greasy oil slick materialized on the surface. Most distressing, the water was a brownish color.

As I heard the family inside starting for the back

door from the condo, I had two choices. I could tell them not to come in and spend some time cleaning out the hot tub, or I could run over and turn the jets back on so they wouldn't see the grime they were sitting in. Being the male that I am, you can guess what I did. I turned the jets back on and didn't say a word.

If you are disgusted, I am sorry. I did clean it the next morning. But the story makes a good point, don't you think? We all have stuff going on in our lives that we really should clean out and work on. But instead we just keep on at an out-of-control pace, too busy to stop. Then one day we wonder why life seems to be falling apart. Maybe your problem isn't the job or the spouse or the kids but the busyness that has helped cause the brokenness in your life.

Do we all relocate to Montana and live in a commune? I suppose that could work. But the answer for most of us isn't to move away from our problems. It's to stop the frantic pace, make some healthy adjustments, apply a major dose of discipline, and find a healthier pace.

Have you ever seen the road sign that reads, "Speed Kills"? Of course it's referring to driving too fast, but I'm convinced that phrase also relates to the pace of life we often live. For many of us, it's just too fast and busy. I don't know about you, but when I'm living at an unsustainable pace, I experience emotional numbness and exhaustion. And like driving too fast, that's when we are prone to make relational, emotional, and even lifestyle mistakes. At the same time, I get it. Sometimes we are going to have a really busy season. Maybe it's a deadline at work or innumerable family activities and commitments. There may come a season when a loved one is ill or needs extra time and attention. But if we are always living at 110 percent, we will never have the margin to add healthiness to our lives. The results of a constantly busy lifestyle are not attractive. I like what Vince Lombardi, the great football coach of the Green Bay Packers, once said: "Fatigue makes cowards of us all." I know that when I'm dangerously tired and fatigued, I'm a lousy husband, father, and leader. Here are just a few effects of what some would call the "hurry sickness syndrome":

- *Loss of rhythm.* I'm not talking about dance moves or I'd be in big trouble. I'm talking about practicing the healthy daily, weekly, and monthly rhythms that bring wholeness to our souls and our relationships. When there is no healthy sustainable rhythm in our lives, we tend to get our priorities out of order. When my rhythm is off, I find myself dealing with emotional numbness in my relationships and my choices. Constant busyness, just like that filthy hot tub, is a sign that our lives are out of control and we need to clean out whatever is keeping us at an unsustainable pace.

- *Loss of physical and relational healthiness.* A busy life often means we aren't taking care of our health needs. I can usually recognize that my life is overcrowded when I quit taking care of my physical needs. Some of the most successful people I know still find time to take care of their bodies by staying in shape. Whenever I speak to parents about replenishing their lives and I mention healthy lifestyle choices, they totally understand that their busyness is partly to blame for their poor health and can also be the cause of their kids' risky behaviors. One woman who was struggling with her physical and marital health said it this way: "I ran too far, too long on too many borrowed miles, and then it hit me like something just plain awful. I've been a psychological, spiritual, and emotional mess. I need to refine my life, my marriage, and my parenting so I can live again." Being dangerously tired goes hand in hand with the lessened ability to say no to risky behaviors. We must ask, "Is the pace of my life sustainable?" If it's not, we need to make some changes and not risk waiting until something breaks down.

- *Loss of spiritual focus.* In a constantly busy life, one of the first things we lose is any kind of deeper spiritual connection. We are just too busy to gain strength from God. Someone once said, "You can't draw water from an empty well." Today, more and more research proves the profound relationship between a breakneck pace and a loss of spiritual well-being for individuals and for families. We can so easily become people (or families) who are over-committed and underconnected. As I reflected on my life after my cancer scare, I realized I was overcommitted to doing some good things, but I didn't like where my primary relationships were headed. Our primary relationships are our relationships with God, family, and even our own souls. If you are too busy for spiritual focus and spiritual discipline, then you are just too busy.

Do you ever experience any of those losses? I haven't found an easy answer to this tendency to be overcommitted and underconnected, but I have found a simple one. (And there *is* a difference between simple and easy.) It's one word: rest.

In the beautiful Hebrew language, the word for rest is sabbath. Sabbath is more of a lifestyle choice than taking a nap or a day off to get some things done around the house. Sabbath living is the con-stant choice to live with margin in our lives. Margin is the space between our load and our limits. Margin is our mental, emotional, and spiritual strength. It's our reserves, our breathing room, our energy, our vitality. Unfortunately, few of us have much margin in our lives. Dr. Richard Swenson says it this way:

"The unbalanced life will not be kind to us in the area neglected."[9] When our lives have margin, it means we are doing the work to bring a sense of rest and wholeness to our bodies, minds, and souls.

Are you overloaded? You may already know whether overload syndrome is plaguing your life and family, but these questions can help you assess:

1. Have you stopped enjoying life because you are too busy?
2. Have you stopped developing new relationships?
3. Are you exhausted most of the time?
4. If you're married, do you and your spouse have a regular date night?
5. Does your family have an enjoyable dinner together on a regular basis?
6. Do you get enough sleep?
7. Do you regularly take a restful day off?
8. Do you often take a break from social media and emails?
9. Do you have credit problems or a large debt load?
10. Are your children showing signs of stress?

If you answered yes to most of these questions, you are experiencing overload. Read on for some things you can do.

After my cancer episode, I decided to build more rest into my life. I remember reading God's instructions to Moses and the Israelites about observing the Sabbath: "It is a sign between Me and the children of Israel forever; for in six days the LORD made the heavens and the earth, and on the seventh day, He rested and was refreshed" (Ex. 31:17 NKJV). I didn't totally understand that verse until I studied the words rested and refreshed. Why would God need to rest and be refreshed?

I now look at those words as a prescription for our lives. The word refreshed can also be translated to mean "exhale." God took a breath. Are you intentional about finding times of rest and refreshment? When I realized I needed to make some changes in my life and that it was time for me to take the lead in my family with this new direction of not being overcommitted, I wrote down four words in my journal: rest, refresh, restore, and recreate. For me, these words are all a part of living a sabbath life. Today, I would call sabbath a prescription to fight the sickness of busyness and hurry.

Rest. I've asked people all over the world this question: "Do you and your family stop the busy pace of life to take a restful, peaceful break?" Most of the time I hear, "I wish we did, but we don't very often." Americans are guilty of not even taking a reasonable amount of vacation, let alone a weekly time of rest. If you are not taking a twenty-four-hour restful break each week, you are probably pressing toward burnout. Emotionally, physically, and mentally healthy people know how to rest. They work hard but understand the importance of a day off. They regularly rest from social media and phones and other distractions. To put rest into our schedules is to find replenishment for our hurried souls, and the only way to do that is to cease too much activity. Rest is a discipline that brings recovery to our lives.

Refresh. What do you do regularly to recharge and rejuvenate? What do you do to refresh your family relationships? Everyone is different, but we all need permission to do whatever it takes to refresh our souls and our primary relationships. For one family I know, Monday evening is sacred. They go out for ice cream and then come home and play a game together. My wife gets refreshed by taking a long hike. Someone else will become refreshed by curling up next to the fire and reading a good novel. Years ago, when I was a pastor in a church, my body was often in need of a peaceful and restorative nap on Sunday afternoon. If you've been overloaded a while, it may take some effort to find what works for you, but do whatever it takes to find refreshment.

Restore. Cancer woke me up to the fact that our lives and relationships bend and break under the burden of busyness. Repair and rebuilding come from proactively restoring our lives. What do you do regularly to restore your soul and your relationships? For Cathy and me, it's a date night each week. I have some friends who are high-profile, extremely busy leaders. No doubt their busyness has added a lot of conflict in their relationship. I suggested they attend an intensive marriage experience, spending four nights and five days in rigorous counseling and communication. I thought it might be the difference between divorce and reconciliation. I warned them it would cost thousands of dollars. I met with them about a month after they returned from the marriage intensive and asked them what was the most insightful decision of the experience. "We now walk our dog twice around the block and talk together every night," they said. I wanted to say, "That's it?" Then they added, "We hadn't been spending much time together, so we never really restored our relationship. Now the first time around the block is dealing with whatever issue might be on our minds between us, and the second time around is to restore the relationship." They were effusive in praising me for giving them the idea. It works for them. I could have told them to walk their dog together for nothing and it could have saved them thousands of dollars! Again, do whatever works for you. And usually you know what you need to do to rebuild and restore.

Recreate. Yes, recreation is a form of rest. Is there enough recreation in your life? The healing element of lesson 1, "Have Serious Fun," is in the fact that play often causes deep soul rest. Recreation together creates a bond in families like few other experiences. Here are three benefits of adding more recreation to your life:

1. *You unplug from the daily grind.* It takes your mind off whatever is stressing you and adds the fun factor to your life.
2. *It improves your health.* Participating in physical activity enhances your muscles, helps with sleep issues, decreases stress, and produces what I like to call the "feel-good hormones," which give you a better quality of life.
3. *It improves bonding.* Most recreation is done together, and this produces healthy conversations, which in turn produce wholesome bonding with others.

I love what John Mark Comer has written on the discipline of rest. He didn't make it sound easy, but he made it sound right. We tend to have a relentless lust for more and for staying busy. "Don't buy. Don't sell. Don't shop. Don't surf the web. . . . Just put all that away and enjoy. Drink deeply from the well of ordinary life: a meal with friends, time with family, a walk in the forest, afternoon tea. Above all, slow down long enough to enjoy life with God, who offers everything that materialism promises but can never deliver on— namely, contentment."[10] Enough said, drop the mic.

Pause long enough to "be still and know" that God is in that stillness, that he longs to heal you and bring you perspective. Remember that our brokenness often comes out of our busyness. If you've noticed busyness creeping up on you, get together with your family and your people and make some healthy changes.

PRACTICE POSITIVE ADAPTABILITY

*The measure of intelligence
is the ability to change.*
—ALBERT EINSTEIN

This principle has been right at the top of important life lessons for me in the last few years.
One of the most frequently asked questions I get is,
"What ingredients make a successful relationship?"
Like so many of the lessons in this book, the answer
sounds simple, but it's not always easy. I don't think
anyone really believes there is a magic wand or secret
formula that will give you a successful relationship.
Relationships can be complicated. But there are two

words that rise above other words and actions. These words make the difference in the best of marriages, families, and work environments. They are especially helpful in improving a relationship that has become high maintenance or is struggling. These two words are *positive adaptability*.

As I investigated happy, healthy relationships, particularly in marriages and families, patterns emerged. If people lived by the patterns of positive adaptability, their relationships seemed to thrive, and if people didn't, their relationships struggled and fell apart. The people who were doing well still seemed to have many of the same problems as those who weren't. They had similar conflicts, tensions, and challenges. The difference was in their attitude about those circumstances.

Adaptability

I was in Hollywood sitting in the beautiful high-rise office of marriage expert and founder of eharmony .com Dr. Neil Clark Warren. Over the years, Neil had become a strong mentor for me in the field of relationships. I asked him, "What is the most important trait of a healthy, vibrant relationship?" Without a moment's hesitation, he gave me a one-word answer: adaptability. One of the few things you can count on in any relationship is change. Whether or not you choose it, change will happen. Staying married, having children, buying a home, navigating health issues, changing jobs, dealing with the poor choices of a family member, and addressing whatever else gets you in the pit of your stomach requires adaptability. Dr. Warren said, "If I could give one gift to every couple on their wedding day, I'd wrap up a large box filled with adaptability. Because no matter how good your relationship is, you will have to be flexible enough to change yourself and at least tolerate your partner's differences."

Cathy and I have been married for forty-six years, and we are very different from each other. We tend to drive each other crazy. I'm an extrovert, and she is an introvert. She is detailed, and I'm . . . let's just say not as detailed. I'm the eternal optimist, and she isn't negative, but she is more of a realist. I try to be on time to things, and Cathy typically runs late. There is a principle that has helped us to embrace our differences. I promise that if you apply it to most aspects of life, it makes a major difference. Here it is: ask yourself, "Does it really matter?" Maybe you've recognized this already, but most things really don't matter. Some do, but not everything matters as much as we tend to think it does in the moment.

Let's apply this principle to the important issue of sharing a tube of toothpaste. Let's pretend that your spouse squeezes the tube from the middle (yuck), and you neatly roll the tube from the bottom the way—may I humbly add—Jesus would. Does it really matter? Of course it doesn't. Buy two tubes of toothpaste and get past it. Life has enough complications not to be hassled by things that don't matter.

In the words of Winston Churchill, "You will never reach your destination if you stop and throw stones at every dog that barks." It goes back to the principle learned in lesson 3: your circumstances may not change, but your attitude can, and that makes all the difference in the world.

As a writer and communicator, I love the stories of people who overcome difficult times and continue to thrive—people, heroes really, who had the courage to become adaptable in a difficult situation. One of those favorite stories for me comes from a surgeon named Richard Selzer. It speaks for itself.

I stand by the bed where a young woman lies, her face postoperative, her mouth twisted in palsy, clownish. A tiny twig of the facial nerve, the one to the muscles of her mouth, has been severed. She will be thus from now on. The surgeon had followed with religious fervor the curve of her flesh; I promise you that. Nevertheless, to remove the tumor in her cheek, I had cut the little nerve.

Her young husband is in the room. He stands

on the opposite side of the bed, and together they seem to dwell in the evening lamplight, isolated from me, private. Who are they, I ask myself, he and this wry-mouth I have made, who gaze at and touch each other so generously, greedily? The young woman speaks.

"Will my mouth always be like this?" she asks.

"Yes," I say, "it will. It is because the nerve was cut."

She nods, and is silent. But the young man smiles.

"I like it," he says. "It is kind of cute."

All at once I *know* who he is. I understand, and I lower my gaze. One is not bold in an encounter with a god. Unmindful, he bends to kiss her crooked mouth, and I so close I can see how he twists his own lips to accommodate to hers, to show her that their kiss still works.[11]

What a beautiful illustration of adapting to a difficult situation with grace and creativity.

When I was younger and much less aware of the value of an eternal perspective, more things mattered. Today, after facing my mortality, adaptability has become much more important to me. Almost every day, I hear my inner voice saying, "Does it really matter?" And most of the time, it really doesn't.

Positivity

Positivity is the twin of adaptability. Positivity is the emotional climate of a healthy relationship. Dr. John Gottmann, one of the world's leading experts on relationships, claims that one of the major differences between a stable relationship and an unstable one is the positivity you have toward your spouse or kids or family members or coworkers. As it turns out, positivity is a choice. It's about learned optimism, and that becomes a powerful trait in any relationship. Gottmann created what he calls the Magic Ratio. He found in his research that five positive interactions to one negative interaction make relationships significantly more likely to succeed. He says he has never seen a marriage fail with that ratio, and that a marriage often is doomed if the ratio drops down to one positive interaction to one negative interaction.

Negativity in a relationship or in your mindset is seldom good. Negativity can kill a relationship quicker than a wildfire. This may sound like an oversimplification, but a habitual mindset of negativity can devour the happiness of any relationship like few issues can. Flee from it. Philippians 2:14 says, "Do everything without grumbling or arguing." My experience is that grumblers and complainers are unhappy people who do much more poorly in relationships and in life. If you constantly think negatively, your thoughts become self-fulfilling prophecies. "As he thinks in his heart, so is he" (Prov. 23:7 NKJV). It was Emerson who said, "We become what we think about all day long."

Problems versus Patterns

Typically, a problem is much easier to solve than a pattern. If you can figure out how to solve your problem, it can usually be resolved by following your plan. Patterns, on the other hand, are more difficult.

My wife uses the term muscle memory default. She has taught me that our thoughts and actions are closely tied to our brain reflex reactions. By programming positivity into our brain muscle, it becomes our memory default.

Do you know your negativity pattern? Your negativity triggers? How about your negativity blind spots? When you figure out what causes your muscle memory to default toward negativity, it's much easier to reprogram your mind for a more positive response. The recovery movement taught me a simple way to recognize my triggers with the letters HALT. They remind me that when I'm hungry, angry, lonely, or tired, I need to HALT and take care of that problem so I don't default to negativity. At the same time, taking care of my mind, body, spirit, and relationships is what keeps me from needing to HALT so much.

If we don't take care of our negativity patterns, we can easily begin to exhibit habitual ugliness and eventually become an awfulizer.

Have you ever known an awfulizer? It can happen to anyone. When we get into a negative mind space, we tend to awfulize—to "imagine (a situation) to be as bad as it can possibly be."[12] My daughter Becca has a master's degree in clinical psychology and taught me this word, a recent addition to the dictionary.

Most of us know an awfulizer:

- "My husband is late from work again. He's probably having an affair."
- "Our son is such a flirt, he's going to impregnate most of the girls in his class."
- "We will *never* get out of debt."
- "We will *never* get along."

Awfulizers drive themselves and others crazy with negative thoughts, damaging themselves and their relationships. Awfulizers tend to be unhappy and unfulfilled people.

If you tend toward awfulizing, do whatever it takes to figure out the cause—usually a big disappointment or loss—and get help talking it out. Replacing awfulizing with positivity can help too. But it can take some time to replace an ingrown habit. Acknowledge the strain and accept the need to find someone to listen and help you unpack your heartsick feelings. And if you are in a position to help an awfulizer, pray and consider how best to help. No one said it would be easy, but it is possible. When life comes unhinged, we can't control all of our thoughts. But that makes it all the more important to control the thoughts that are manageable, and to connect with a good listener to get help dealing with the rest.

At the end of the Sermon on the Mount, Jesus gave a relevant illustration about home building, but it was more of a life lesson. To summarize, he said some people build their homes on rock and others build them on sand. When the wind, rain, and storms come (and they will, they always do), the home with the rock foundation will last because it was built on bedrock, but the home built on sand will collapse with a mighty crash. Everyone experiences tough times, and how we build our lives makes the difference in whether we crash or make it through the storm as better people.

Negativity is the default way. It's the undisciplined way. And it doesn't work. Choosing positive adaptability takes more work, but the results are so much better. Shifting your perspective to build your life and relationships on positive adaptability is building your house on solid rock. And when the rains come down and the floods come up, you'll be able to keep your footing. I promise you won't regret it.

Lesson 6

IT'S THE PAIN OF DISCIPLINE OR THE PAIN OF REGRET

> *Great leaders always have self-discipline—without exception.*
>
> —JOHN C. MAXWELL

My arms are sore and my chest is tight today. It's not from a heart issue. I'm working out. I've lost eleven pounds, and I'm going for nine more in the next few months. If you looked at me, your first thought would not be, "Wow, that guy is a stud!" But the soreness and the loss of weight make me feel like I'm progressing.

The other day I said to one of my daughters, "Look at my arms!" (Okay, I was a little proud.) "That's the pain of discipline." Then I grabbed my love handles and said, "This is the pain of regret!" The way I figure it, there is pain in life no matter what, and when you simplify it, making wise choices is often about choosing the pain of discipline over the pain of regret. I have no idea what caused my cancer, but I do know that eating better is a good thing. So I decided that the pain of discipline was going to be to eat more like my wife does.

Talk about a disciplined eater! I have teased her for most of our marriage about what she eats and doesn't eat, but she also is in great shape. So now most mornings I eat plain Greek yogurt and granola with berries, and for lunch, a salad with very lite dressing. Can I let you in on a secret? I don't like plain Greek yogurt and I'm not really a salad guy, but I've grown to appreciate how eating them makes me feel. It's not that I hate those foods. It's just that I like pancakes, waffles, and cheesy omelets better. (Oh, I'm getting hungry just thinking about those.) A burger and fries is just plain better than a salad, a hundred times out of a hundred. But what I like more is not experiencing the pain of regret.

The same principle works for relationships, work, and our spiritual lives. We almost always know what to do. We just don't want to do it. To be honest, you and

I are "experts" on a lot of subjects, but we just don't follow our own wisdom. The apostle Paul gave some great advice to his protege Timothy: "Discipline yourself for the purpose of godliness" (1 Tim. 4:7 NASB). Paul chose a word for discipline that has athletic undertones. I think he was trying to explain to his younger mentee that if you want to live a fulfilled life of spiritual purpose and integrity, it takes the discipline of an athlete. As a Christian, I firmly believe in God's grace and unmerited favor. But keeping our relationship with him flourishing takes some good old-fashioned discipline on our part. Frankly, it takes discipline to keep any relationship flourishing.

In 1983, I was sitting in my bedroom having some quiet time with God. I wish I could say that happened every day. It didn't. I was unfocused and had high hopes for spending time with God, but it didn't happen consistently. That morning I found myself telling God that I would like to give him two hours a day. I had heard that was what Billy Graham did, and I had known a Korean pastor in graduate school who gave God 10 percent of his day for prayer and Bible reading. But as those words came out of my mouth, I knew I would fail.

I realized I was not exactly Billy Graham, and as much as I respected my Korean friend, I had way too much adult ADD to sit still for two hours. So I started to say I'd spend one hour each day, but I knew that would also be setting myself up for failure. Okay, I admit it. I can get easily distracted. So in the quietness of my bedroom, I said, "God, I would like to commit to twenty minutes with you each day." It sounded a bit wimpy, but it also felt right. I have missed some days since then, but as I get older, those missed days happen less and less. I believe the strength I have for doing life well and for being effective with my family and ministry is a direct result of investing those twenty minutes a day.

I don't always remember what I've read or prayed about in those quiet moments, but it still nourishes me for the day. How about you? Do you practice the discipline of spending time with God daily? Maybe it's five minutes instead of twenty. The amount probably doesn't matter as much as the cumulative time spent over days, weeks, months, and years. Discipline creates a habit that becomes a habit of your heart.

I love the story about a day in the life of Jesus found in Luke 6:12–17. To summarize, Jesus spent time in the morning in a quiet place, praying and listening to God (solitude). He then came back and spent time with his disciples. I call those kinds of relationships "replenishing relationships." From his discipline of solitude and time with his replenishing relationships, he was able to do his work. Too often we pour all of our energy into our work and end up giving our families and personal lives emotional scraps because we are so dry from lack of solitude and replenishing relationships. If we aren't careful, it can become a way of life that damages our inner being.

Take a look at the diagram "A Day in the Life of Jesus." It's a great model for all of us to follow.

A Day in the Life of Jesus

Solitude

Community/
Replenishing Relationships

Family/Marriage/Work

Jesus was prepared to do his life work in a much more effective way because he disciplined himself to regularly practice solitude. He went away and prayed. Then he came back and spent time with his disciples, his replenishing community. It doesn't exactly say it in the Bible, but maybe they had a few mud fights by the Sea of Galilee. They definitely supported each other through tougher times. Jesus found strength in the discipline of time with God and his deepened friendships, and this is what gave him the ability to work. I figure that if it's the model Jesus followed, why not the rest of us too?

Through the years many people have asked me, "How do you get the discipline to succeed?" I wish there was an easy answer or a magic formula. We live in such an instant-everything culture, but I have never found an instant plan for the pain of discipline. The best answer I can give you is that it's going to take a lot of grit.

The dictionary meaning of the word grit is "courage and resolve; strength of character." Phrases like *strength of will* and words like fortitude, toughness, determination, and resolution all help to describe having grit in your life. You can't just will or wish change to happen. It takes discipline. Angela Lee Duckworth describes grit this way in one of the most popular TED Talks of all time: "Grit is passion and perseverance for very long-term goals. Grit is having stamina. Grit is sticking with your future, day in, day out, not just for the week, not just for the month, but for years, and working really hard to make that future a reality. Grit is living life like it's a marathon, not a sprint."[13]

For me, grit and discipline lead with this question: "Are you willing to do whatever it takes to bring intimacy to your marriage? Your work? Your health? Your family relationships? Your [fill in the blank]?" If you are willing to do whatever it takes over the long haul, then you are on your way to success. Some have asked me, "What if I give my marriage everything I've got, and it still doesn't work out?" My response is, "Wouldn't it feel better to have given your all than to wonder 'what if'?" I know, grit sounds so unromantic and so unspontaneous when it comes to marriage and relationships, but it's one of the top reasons for marital and relational success. In Duckworth's excellent book, *Grit: The Power of Passion and Perseverance*,[14] she claims that grit is a better predictor of success than intelligence and talent. I think she is right.

Even the Bible speaks about discipline and grit:

- *"Endure patiently"* (Rev. 3:10).
- "Blessed is the one who *perseveres under trial* because, having *stood the test*, that person will receive the crown of life that the Lord has promised" (James 1:12).
- "We want each of you to show this same *diligence* to the very end, so that what you hope for may be fully realized" (Heb. 6:11).
- *"Stand firm*, and you will win life" (Luke 21:19).

All the words in italics are words of grit, and there are some great promises that go along with them.

Perseverance

Much of what I've written about discipline and grit is summed up by the word perseverance. I love studying the biographies of ordinary men and women who made an extraordinary impact on the world. They come from a wide variety of familial, racial, educational, financial, and even creedal backgrounds, but the one thing they all seem to possess is an extra dose of perseverance. I have a friend who grew up poor in the South. His great-grandfather and great-grandmother were slaves. He remembers seeing the mark his great-grandmother bore on her shoulder from a branding iron. My friend has a wonderful family and is incredibly successful in his business. He is generous in his church and a leader in his community. I asked him the secret of his success. Without pausing, he replied, "Staying focused on my priorities and never losing sight of my desired outcomes." When I visited his home one time, I noticed a sign above his desk that read, "First Things First." I asked him about it, and he said, "That sign helps me remember not to get distracted, and there are a lot of 'attractive distractions.'"

He told me a story about an uncle who lives in Africa and is an expert guide who takes people on treks to the top of Mount Kilimanjaro, the world's tallest freestanding mountain and Africa's highest peak. Climbing Kilimanjaro doesn't require any technical skills or special equipment, just some physical fitness and a lot of determination. The one thing his uncle shares with all the people he guides is, "Keep your eyes on the peak." His uncle has found through the years that if a person keeps their eyes on the top, they almost always make it. If they take their eyes off the peak and become distracted, they often will give up before they finish.

Isn't one of the main goals of our lives to finish well? What will it take for you? Again, most of us know the simple answer, we just don't always do it. What will it take to sustain your life, family, and relationships? You know the answer. Don't bail out early. Don't quit. It's never too late to find the discipline to persevere. It's worth the pain and effort to avoid the alternative.

FAMILY MATTERS
MORE THAN WORK

*This is my family. I found it all
on my own. It's little and broken,
but still good. Yeah, still good.*
—STITCH, IN DISNEY'S *LILO AND STITCH*

It seems like this conversation happened just yester-day, but it took place before Cathy and I even had kids. I was a pastor to students at a thriving church in Orange, California, and one night after a great youth-group meeting, we went to get something to eat. As we sat down, Cathy's lip began to quiver. Even though we had been married only a few years, I knew the quivering lip was not a good sign.

She blurted, "Jim, I'm not sure we should have children."

"What on earth are you talking about, Cathy? We talked about our love for kids and our desire to have them on our first date!"

She said, "I know. But you are so busy with your work and spending time with everyone else's kids. I just don't know if you would be present in our kids' lives."

She added, "I feel like you are always working!"

I felt like she had stabbed me in the gut. What's worse, I knew she was right. I loved my work. I loved everything about my job, and more than that, it was going quite well. My self-esteem needs were being met by a growing youth ministry and a church that loved us. At the same time, I knew in my heart that I was working too many hours and that it was affecting my relationship with Cathy and that my work eventually would affect my relationship with our children if I didn't make some changes.

I looked her in the eyes and said, "I'm having an affair!"

Not with another woman. It was with my work, and that affair was stealing much of my focus and attention from Cathy. I had to admit she was getting only my emotional scraps. I was giving my best to my work, and there wasn't much left over for her.

I don't know about you, but I have struggled all my

adult life with confused priorities. And yet, I could tell you what the right priorities should be, even though I've had trouble living them out. Most of the people I know would say their priorities should be:

1. God
2. marriage
3. children
4. vocation

The problem is that we constantly get our priorities muddied. Because I'm in ministry, there have been many times I've gotten my vocation mixed up with my relationship with God. When Cathy and I finally did have children, we found it easy to fall into a child-focused marriage, even though we knew that often makes kids feel entitled and believe they are the center of the universe. And of course, the main result of an out-of-balance, child-focused marriage is lack of connection and intimacy between spouses. One of Cathy's favorite sayings to me was, "Jim, we already have a messiah. He is doing very well. Don't try to replace him."

I'm not saying that work isn't important. I'm just saying that work is not more important than family. I've never heard anyone say toward the end of their life, "I should have worked more hours." I've heard many key leaders say, "If I could change anything, I would have spent more quality time with my family."

Are you giving your family only your emotional scraps? If you don't know the answer, ask your family. They will tell you. Most people I know want a close-knit family. We just don't act like it sometimes with our calendar and priorities. The key is not to prioritize our schedules but to schedule our priorities. This will always ensure that our families get our best attention.

Back to that restaurant with Cathy's lip still quivering and my telling her that work was my mistress. We pulled out a paper napkin and wrote down three priorities for our marriage:

1. *Nonnegotiable date night.* We had gotten away from spending quality time together. She wasn't looking for my attention every moment, but if we could spend one night a week connecting and enjoying each other, that would make a difference. I now ask people whether they are willing to give their spouses just 1 percent of their time each week for a date. That's only 100 minutes out of the 10,080 minutes we have each week.

2. *Out only three nights a week.* This may not be your issue, but I was out of the house many nights working with kids and families, but still working all day as well. We decided that for the health of our relationship and our future family, we would try to be out only three nights a

week. I had to make some major adjustments to my schedule, but it was a big help to our relationship and to our children as they were growing up.

3. *Veto power over my schedule.* Too often I was making scheduling decisions without checking with Cathy. We decided she could have veto power over my travel and calendar. Now we make decisions together, and if we do overcommit, as sometimes happens, it's a mutual decision. No more blaming or shaming. There had been a lot of tension between us over my busy calendar, but with both of us involved in my scheduling, much of that tension was resolved.

What three priorities do you need to think about? When you work to make your family more of a priority with greater emotional connection, almost everything looks brighter.

Overcoming Negative Family Patterns

Until I was a young adult, it never dawned on me that I had come from a dysfunctional family. For the most part, the family system you grow up in is normal for you. No family is perfect, but as I began to understand more about my family, I realized that alcoholism was prevalent. Cathy had similar insight into her not-so-perfect family as well.

As we married and had three incredible daughters, we became more aware that we needed to overcome some negative family patterns to be better parents and spouses. Cathy and I decided to do everything we could to become a transitional generation. The Bible says that you inherit the sin bent of a previous generation, up to the third and fourth generations, but it also says that God lavishes his love on a thousand generations (Ex. 34:6–7 NLT). With that thought in mind, Cathy and I decided to do everything we could to recover and not repeat the negative family patterns from our past. Our issues weren't the same as our families', but the drive for our work and careers was sometimes clouding our connection with each other and our family.

I remember a conversation I had with my oldest daughter when she was seventeen. I'd overheard her talking with her mom about all the ways she was unhappy with our family. It was intense and emotional. She got a little disrespectful, so I stepped in and sent her to her room. She turned on me and then slammed our kitchen door, which has a sign over it that reads, "Bless This House." The sign went crooked, and for several years we just left it that way.

I followed her up to her room and said, "It's my turn to talk." The look on my face had her attention. I said, "Some of the things you said about Mom are true."

She looked at me with an expression that said, "Good, Dad's on my side." Then I said, "And I want you never to talk to my wife like that again." My voice was cool and calm, but I was screaming on the inside. I added, "Furthermore, your mom is the person in my life whom I have seen grow the most. As you can only imagine, she came from quite a dysfunctional family. She started her life with a deficit but has grown so very much."

I told my daughter that long before she was a sparkle in our eyes, we decided to do all we could to recover from our negative family patterns. "And," I said, "that has given you a chance to move farther than your mom or I ever will, if you choose." I never yelled at her, but my words brought tears to her eyes. She knew the sacrifice, courage, and dedication her mom was making to move past the dysfunction toward a healthier life and family. She ended up leaving her room and apologizing to Cathy for her hurtful and unfounded words.

We're all called to be the transitional generation and have a healthier family life than our past. To do that, we first need to admit our brokenness, develop the courage to change, and live with the right priorities.

In Elisabeth Kübler-Ross's research on dying, she noted that people at the end of their lives have two dominant desires: a right relationship with God and a right relationship with their loved ones. Even if they are not particularly religious or don't have close family ties, these become their focus.

When I was recovering from cancer surgery, I had an overwhelming desire not to wait until my death to make those two desires my top priorities. And I knew it wouldn't happen flying by the seat of my pants, making family decisions by circumstance and by chance.

936

Do you know the significance of the number 936? I think about that number almost every day. It helps me put my family priorities in the right order. My friends Kristen Ivy and Reggie Joiner of Orange (a division of the reThink Group) taught me that between a person's birth and launching into adulthood there are only 936 weeks.

I have on my mobile device the Parent Cue app from their organization, which has photos of my grandkids on it and tells me how many weeks of their childhoods are left. Looking at the app makes me want to build into my relationship with them even more with legacy values. My prayer is from a psalm: "Teach us to number our days, that we may gain a heart of wisdom" (Ps. 90:12). Building healthy family relationships doesn't come naturally. It takes intentionality and a plan.

Here is a valuable exercise that might help. Since people support what they help create, I suggest you do this exercise together with your family:

Our Family Plan

Values

What are the timeless values that guide our family?

Purpose

What is the purpose of our family's existence?

When our kids were twelve, ten, and eight, we sat around a campfire in Lake Tahoe, California, and wrote out our "family constitution." Out of this constitution, which stayed on our refrigerator through the teen years, we developed our values and purpose.

Burns Family Constitution

- Honor
- Trust
- Truthfulness and integrity
- Fruit of the Spirit (love, joy, peace, patience, kindness, goodness, faithfulness, gentleness, and self-control)
- Support and encouragement
- Time together
- Sharing and generosity

- Respect
- Following our moral code

The Plan

Three-to-five-year plan: Using your values and purpose, write out your plan to ensure that your purpose is met. Our family plan included ensuring good health, building strong relationships, instilling a healthy spiritual life, engaging in athletics, education, training in sex education, and lessons in marriage, in how to build friendships, and in finding meaningful work.

One-year plan: Take the same areas of your three-to-five-year plan and see what you might instill in your life as a family this year. Keep it doable and meaningful. We tend to overplan for one year and underplan for five years.

Generation to Generation

Now that I'm an older guy and I'm facing my mortality with more of an eternal perspective, I'm thinking a lot about legacy. It's true that we inherit both the good and the not-so-good from previous generations. I love my vocation, but it's my family influence that will last for generations. I now view my main job in life as helping my kids, and now my grandkids, to one day become responsible adults who love God. I can do that by helping them find and invest in their mission (purpose), mate (healthy relationships), and master (God). In my view, if we can have even a small part in that process, it's worth putting our family relationships above our jobs.

Think about what legacy you'd like to pass on to your kids and grandkids. Begin being more intentional about that this very week.

Lesson 8

FIND REPLENISHING RELATIONSHIPS

*Friendship is born at that
moment when one person says
to another, "What! You too? I
thought I was the only one."*

—C. S. LEWIS

Do you have deep friendships? Do you have supportive people in your life, what I call replenishing relationships? They're more important than we tend to think. Dr. Jones was one of my favorite college professors. He used to say, "Most people have tons of acquaintances but very few deep friendships." I think he was quite right about that. Maybe that's as it should be, but all of us can increase our investment in restorative friendships.

A mentor of mine who is also a well-known leader around the world, once confided that he was often lonely. He said, "Many leaders are some of the loneliest people I know." There's something particularly isolating about rising to a position of greater responsibility. Being recognized and appreciated for your contributions is great, but it's not uncommon to find yourself feeling more alone after a promotion. At the same time, I don't think I have ever heard anyone say, "I wish I had fewer deep friendships."

Do you have at least three replenishing relationships? The Bible says there is a friend who sticks closer than a brother or a sister. If you do have a few such deep friendships, you are truly fortunate.

True friends accept you for who you are. They support and encourage you. Friends know your faults and love you anyway. They are caring and affirming but tell you the truth in love, even if it hurts. They don't walk away from you when things are hard. They grieve with you, listen to you, and are willing to sacrifice for you. Friends are a safe place, a continual source of replenishing and restoring.

My wife, Cathy, had that kind of a deep friendship with Carolyn. She went to junior high, high school, and even college with Carolyn. They were the perfect illustration of a deep friendship. Carolyn's husband, Russ, and I used to joke that our wives liked being with each other more than they liked being with us. It was sort of true, but it never bothered me because I knew that when Cathy was in Carolyn's presence or on the phone with her, she came away a better person. They could finish each other's sentences. They often sacrificed time and money to hang out with each other. They shared their joys and were vulnerable with their secrets. They confessed feelings, disappointments, mistakes, and hurts. Yet I never once felt jealous of that relationship because I knew it was so uplifting to them both. They practiced what I would call a Galatians 6:2 relationship: "Carry each other's burdens, and in this way you will fulfill the law of Christ."

In her early fifties, Carolyn learned she had pancreatic cancer, not exactly a great cancer to get if you are going to get it. That last year of Carolyn's life, Cathy flew from Southern California to Seattle nine times to support Carolyn. The night before Carolyn died, Cathy had a hunch that it would happen the next day. She took the earliest flight she could and was reading Psalm 23, Carolyn's favorite psalm, at her bedside as she entered eternity.

Their relationship was a model of deep friendship for me. Many people don't have a deep friendship like that, but don't we all want one?

Seek Replenishing Relationships

After my cancer diagnosis, I thought a lot about friendships. I've been fortunate to have good friends, but I realized that I could easily get distracted and not invest the time to make them deep. I came out of my recovery with a strong desire to seek replenishing relationships. I knew already, but it became an undeniable instinct afterward, that the deepest and most replenishing of relationships don't just show up. You must put energy, time, and focus into those few people who are trustworthy companions and confidants, to deepen those relationships. They don't come instantly.

Most of our friendships are of the more superficial type, acquaintances. These fall on a spectrum from the "wave at the neighbor even though you don't know their name" type to closer acquaintances.

Acquaintances tend to be one of two types: VDPs and VIPs. VDPs are very draining people. No doubt a name or two just entered your brain. These could be family members, coworkers, or your spouse's best friend—anyone who, when you spend time with them, you cringe. Some VDPs you can't escape or ignore, and you learn to manage them with boundaries. But we're not here to focus on them.

Acquaintances who can change your life for the better are the VIPs, very important people. These are the ones you need to consider investing more in, people who are your potential replenishing relationships. These are the life-giving people you are already investing some time in, who build you up and make you feel good.

I've had two men in my life like this, John and Jon.

My good friend John Watson recently passed away, but he was one of those replenishing relationships for me. I remember early in my marriage telling Cathy that I wished I could spend time with someone like John more often. She said, "Why don't you eat a meal together or share coffee on a regular basis with him?" I remember saying to her, "John is busy, and besides, he has a lot of relationships in his life where he fills that role." As I look back on that conversation, I understand that I was deciding for John that he was too busy and wouldn't want to meet with me without my ever talking it over with him. Cathy gently nudged me to seek him out, as only a wife can do.

John and I worked at the same church. I happened to run into him soon after my conversation with Cathy. I asked if he would be open to getting lunch. He jumped at the opportunity. That special connection lasted for three years after we began having lunch together every Wednesday. It turned out that while I had assumed that John was too busy to hang out and that his relationship bucket was full, in fact he was looking for the same type of deeper friendship. Even after John moved to another city, our relationship stayed strong, and whenever we got together, we picked up right where we had left off. Today, I am so glad that Cathy pushed me out of my comfort zone to spend time with John. It took effort, but it was well worth it. How about you? Is there someone in your life you'd like to spend time with regularly? Maybe all you need to do is ask.

The other Jon and I met in college. Again, a great guy who was busy and was living a full life. For most of forty years, we got together for a few hours every six weeks. He became the president of a university about an hour away from my house, and for many of those years we met halfway. In that relationship, we tended to walk through a list of accountability questions that were tough but always seemed to bring more clarity and integrity, along with grace and support. I found that talking through our commitments and goals was always so replenishing. When I woke from my cancer surgery, Cathy was talking with Jon. He had sat with her during the entire surgery.

After my recovery, Jon invited me to speak to the university's students at their convocation. He introduced me, and then I looked out at the crowd and said, "My hope for you all is that you find one friend like I have in Jon." I looked at him and remembered a quote by an artist named Flavia Weedn. "Some people come into our lives and quickly go away," I said. "And some stay and leave footprints in our hearts, and we are never, ever the same." I prepared to move into my message, but they started applauding and wouldn't let me speak for a long time. It was humbling and surprising. Later, I reflected on the emotion of the audience, and it dawned on me that these students had a deep appreciation for their president. They saw in him what I saw in him. But also, some of the emotion was their deep desire to experience the rare value of a lifelong replenishing relationship. In that moment onstage, the students saw what they yearned for themselves, a friendship that two older guys had found simply by doing the work to make it happen.

An old Russian proverb says, "Tell me who your friend is, and I will tell you who you are." This is true of all of us.

As you seek deeper friendships, you can find them in three types of replenishing relationships: receiving mentoring, being a peer, and mentoring another.

Receiving Mentoring

Do you have mentors? Are there people in your life to whom you can look for guidance, coaching, wisdom, and wise counsel? If you are married, do you have a couple (or a few couples) you can spend time with periodically who not only provide you with insight but also provide an example of a vibrant marriage? Most successful people mention a mentor who helped them get to where they wanted to go. Moms need older, wiser mentor moms who can provide a listening ear and support. And anyone who leads people needs someone who knows the challenges of that work. Who are your mentors? If you don't have one, make a list of some VIP acquaintances you might pursue today. You won't start by asking them to be your mentor. You can just make an appointment with them and spend time with them, asking a few questions. Show interest and support, and set another date to connect again. See what happens from there as you build a relationship.

Being a Peer

We were never meant to do life, marriage, or parenting alone. Do you have a group of friends who support you and encourage you?

Cathy and I were in a couples' group in our church for many years when our kids were young. That group became a lifeline of support and encouragement. They were a major part of our social life, and we deepened our friendships week by week. Today, the four men I have spent time with every Tuesday morning for more than seventeen years are a lifeline of peer replenishment. I know I am a better husband, father, and president of HomeWord because of my regular encounters with these men. We can share most anything about our lives, we have fun together, and we hold each other accountable. They can ask me the tough questions, and I can ask the same of them.

One morning, I was sharing that I felt like my schedule was out of control with speaking, travel, and administration at my office. One of the men smiled and asked, "Who determines your schedule?" I looked at him and answered, "I do." He smiled again and said, "So what's wrong with your self-image that you need to say yes to so many things that it's getting in the way of your quality of life?"

Ouch. I've never forgotten his gentle rebuke. That's a picture of someone being an incredible encouragement for me. That's a replenishing peer relationship.

Mentoring Another

Are there people in your life who look to you as a mentor? Although I'm not out seeking to be a mentor to others, the mentoring relationships that have come my way have helped me greatly. Being a mentor helps hold you accountable to the principles and lifestyle you consider most important by ensuring you share them as an example with others. This is powerful.

Some mentor relationships are more formal, like what you might experience with an apprentice at work, while others are more casual or spontaneous. Some mentoring is designed to be temporary, and some is lifelong. You can be a mentor to a family member or even an older person, depending on what the connection is.

When my wife was a mentor for a group of young moms in our church, she always came back from that experience radiant. Her connection with them was loose, but many just needed an older, wiser, experienced mom in their lives to reassure them they were going to make it. No matter what the experience of mentoring is for you, being a mentor will often bring a depth of replenishment and encouragement that you didn't expect.

I know few people who feel qualified to be a mentor. The best marriage mentors, life mentors, and sponsors in a recovery program are the people who know they aren't perfect but are willing to share with vulnerability their lives and experience. I always tell younger people looking for a mentor to take a chance. The same goes for being a mentor: take a chance.

A few years ago, our ministry invited my friend and mentor John Watson and his wonderful wife, Barbara, to our annual fundraising benefit. We flew them in from San Antonio, Texas, and they had no idea why we were bringing them to the event. During the presentation, I stood up in front of the crowd and showed a photo of John on the jumbo screen. I said,

"This is John, one of the most influential people in my life and one of my main replenishing relationships. When I was young, he mentored me. I wanted to be like John, have a family like John, be the kind of person John was to me. John's relationship with me changed my life."

At that point, my colleague, coworker, and great friend Doug Fields walked on stage. I handed him a baton. He turned to the crowd and said, "I met Jim when I was in junior high school. He mentored me. I wanted to be like him, have a family like him, imitate the way he treated people. My relationship with Jim changed my life." Then Matt McGill walked on stage and took the baton from Doug. He tried to say something similar to what Doug and I had said, but he started crying. By this time, the entire crowd seemed to be wiping their eyes, including me on stage. Finally, through his tears Matt said, "Doug met me when I was in high school. My relationship with Doug changed my life." We repeated that seven times. The last young man was a young junior high student. He referred to the college student on the stage whose mentoring relationship had touched his life, and then he said, "I also want to thank John Watson for taking a chance to influence and impact Jim Burns and the rest of this lineup." I asked John and Barbara to stand as we presented them with a small token of appreciation. Little did John know that by investing in me, one day toward the end of his life he would see seven more generations of mentoring and life change as a result of his mentoring.

I often tell people to lean into relationships that are replenishing for them and into those that replenish others. Surround yourself with VIPs who bring out the best in you and become a VIP yourself. The book of Proverbs says, "Iron sharpens iron" (27:17). It doesn't just happen. Seek those people out and find time in your busy schedule to invest in those replenishing relationships. You'll never regret it.

SEEK ACCOUNTABILITY FOR EFFECTIVENESS

*If you hang out with chickens, you're
going to cluck, and if you hang out
with eagles, you're going to fly.*

—STEVE MARABOLI

I still remember what street I was driving on when I heard on the radio that one of my heroes had resigned from a major leadership position because of a moral failure. I was devasted. This may sound horrible, but I'm usually not that surprised by moral failure. This time I was shocked. This man had taught me principles to safeguard my life. Obviously, no one is perfect and all of us can move quickly down a slippery slope of poor choices.

One of the fears I have seldom voiced over the years as I have watched people crash and burn morally is that I too might find it easy to compromise my values. This man's hypocritical lifestyle really shook me. Right after hearing the news, I happened to get a call from my friend Henry Cloud. I told him what I had just heard. He also was deeply saddened.

I asked Henry, "What on earth would cause him to make such a poor choice?"

Henry's answer was simple yet profound. "Jim, we all have a dark side. I bet he wasn't in touch with his, and he probably shared his pain and darkness with no one."

I found out later that was exactly what had happened. Here was a man with high morals and values and incredible influence. Yet he was accountable to no one. And somehow years of no accountability had brought him to some poor decisions that cost him his life work, his marriage, and his family relationships.

Do you have a safe place to share your hurts, worries, pain, joys, hopes, and goals? Is there someone, or a small group of people, with whom you can be totally honest about your life and who can hold you accountable for your actions? Do you have a safe place to share your life? If the answer is yes, you are most fortunate. Most people move away from transparency in relationships. Brené Brown says it so well: "Vulnerability is the birthplace of love, belonging, joy, courage, empathy, and creativity. It is the source of hope, empathy, accountability, and authenticity. If we want greater clarity in our purpose or deeper and more meaningful spiritual lives, vulnerability is the path."[15]

Think of an accountability relationship as healing and profitable for a successful life. The Bible makes an intriguing statement when it says, "Therefore confess your sins to each other and pray for each other so that you may be healed" (James 5:16). Notice that through honesty and confession, we may be healed. When we think of healing, we sometimes think of dramatic stories and miracles that almost are beyond explanation, but isn't it also true that when we confess our lives through vulnerability to a friend, it often brings healing? That has been my experience.

Accountability Is Security

Over the years, I have allowed individuals in my life to hold me accountable. It has never been easy, and even now, I desire to make myself look better than I am. Which only highlights my need for fresh healing through accountability.

We tend to want to keep ourselves hidden and safe from accountability, but sharing the truth about ourselves with someone we trust is the only way to ensure our safety and security.

Consider just two examples.

Two men get together for coffee before work once a week. They both have struggled with an addiction to pornography. When they see each other, a high five means they have done well and accomplished their goal of not watching any kind of porn. A low five means they need to talk. One of them has messed up again. At the beginning of their relationship, there were a lot more low fives than high fives. But for the last two years, they have given each other only high fives. They still get together to check in every week.

A small group of women meets regularly to talk about life, study inspirational messages, and hold each other accountable. One woman is working on her weight and exercise plan, while another is asking them to hold her accountable to work on the romance in her marriage. They all have different issues but share similar needs and goals. The accountability is their safeguard, their security. In these relationships, there are deepening friendships but also grace and forgiveness, cheerleading, mourning, and celebration.

These are healthy people. Not perfect but growing.

Accountability Breeds Responsibility

I'm so grateful for a small group of men who know me and are willing to hold me accountable. I've been in this group of men for the past seventeen years, and before that, there were other small groups. I'm a better husband and father because of these men. How about you? If you don't have an accountability system in place, step out in faith to grab a person or a group and begin the process. You will be better off in so many ways. A wise mentor told me when I was very young, "Accountability is the measure of a leader's height." I think that is the case for all people.

Developing accountability looks different for everyone. There is no correct way to do it. I have a friend who speaks weekly to his best friend on the phone, and they work through some questions. Others meet around a table at a restaurant and share their issues. There are support groups, recovery groups, Bible studies, and a hundred other ways to invite accountability. It's not a program, it's a process of sharing your life with another human being or group, feeling trusted, supported, and, yes, sometimes challenged. Such relationships don't happen overnight. They grow over time.

My support group took years to become comfortable with vulnerable accountability. As typical guys, we found it easy to talk about sports, politics, business, faith, and our families, but when it came time to share a need or a hurt or even a sin, that was tough. All of us have bailed out at one time or another and taken the easier road of silence. Then one day, one of the men in my group opened his soul to discuss some hurts in his marriage. It was the most remarkable experience. No one preached at him or lectured him about what he was doing wrong. We listened. And listening is the language of love. Sure, we gave some challenging advice, but mainly we created a safe place for him to share. The next week, he shared again, and as time went on, we all began sharing on a deeper level. His vulnerability and willingness to share his shame and hurt became a healing spot for us all. In confessing our pain and joys, there is healing.

Guard Your Heart

As I've studied what truly healthy people or marriages or leaders look like, I've found that it always comes back to the condition of the heart. According to Hebrews, your heart is the center of your being. In the Bible, the words heart and soul are often used interchangeably. Your heart is the center of your physical, emotional, intellectual, and moral activity. So obviously, at all costs we need to guard our hearts. Physically we can guard our hearts by monitoring the food we eat, the exercise we do, the stress we live under, and the chemicals we put into our bodies. But of course there is another side to guarding our hearts, and that involves our actions and choices and, yes, accountability. One of the most important proverbs of all time is "Guard your heart above all else, for it determines the course of your life" (Prov. 4:23 NLT).

Let me explain it this way:

- "Above all else" = your priorities
- "Guard your heart" = your healthy life action plan
- "For it determines the course of your life" = the results of your priorities and plan

If you have right priorities and live by a solid life action plan, the results will be good. Misplaced priorities or lack of an excellent plan or accountability leads to poor results. That's the case for our lives, our relationships, and our vocations. It sounds like an oversimplification, but doesn't it make sense?

No doubt for all of us, obstacles can get in the way:

- Busyness
- Conflict
- Anger, bitterness, or resentment
- Being unfocused on top priorities
- Letting others rob us of joy

- Baggage from the past
- Being negative
- Lack of replenishing relationships
- Money problems
- Addictions, abuse, adultery

Make your own list. One thing we all have in common is that we all have stuff in our lives to deal with, and an accountability relationship can help us move past our obstacles and toward our best lives.

Whenever I speak with people, and particularly leaders, they want to know what types of questions someone can ask in accountability relationships. As I mentioned, accountability relationships come in all shapes and sizes. Here is the list that my friend Jon and I walked through regularly for many years:

- Is it working? Is life working?
- Am I focused on the right things?
- What do I need to do to sustain my life, family, health, and ministry over the long haul? How am I doing? What's holding me back?
- Is my character submitted to Christ?
- Am I living a life of integrity?
- Is my pace of life sustainable?
- Is my heart for God shrinking or growing?
- In what areas of my life do I need the courage to change? What's holding me back?

- Do I have enough replenishing relationships? Do I invest regularly in those relationships?
- Do I like the person I am becoming?
- Is the work of God I'm doing destroying the work of God in me?
- Am I giving my family only my emotional scraps?

I always suggest that people start with an established list but eventually create their own.

There is a fascinating story in the Old Testament of a battle between the Israelites and the Amalekites (Ex. 17:8–13). The battle began with the Amalekites' unprovoked attack on Israel. Moses urged his people to fight back. Under the leadership of Joshua, the man who eventually took over Moses' leadership, the Israelites prepared for battle, and Moses took his place at the top of the hill with his staff in hand. The staff or "rod of God" was often used to do something great for God. As the battle raged on, Moses held up the staff and the Israelites began to win. But Moses became tired and lowered the staff, and the Amalekites gained the advantage. So Moses did a most brilliant act. He asked others to help him hold up the staff. He sat on a rock and the others held his hands up. With the help of those around him, the staff remained above his head and the Israelites won the battle.

Moses knew he couldn't do his part on his own. He

admitted his weakness and weariness and, with the help of others, did his part to win the battle. Not only is this a great story, it's an illustration of the power of others coming alongside Moses to do battle together. That's exactly what accountability can do for your life.

COMMUNICATE WITH AWE

*I cannot blame them for what I
do with what they do to me. I am
responsible for how I respond.*
—Dr. Henry Cloud

Often the difference between a good life and a
lousy life, a thriving relationship and a bad one,
a deeply connected family and a disaster family, is
our ability to communicate. Here's some good news
that was shared with me by one of my mentors, Neil
Clark Warren: "Good communication is a learned
trait." That statement is a game-changer. You can't
blame your family heritage or your spouse, your kids
or your coworkers for how poorly you communicate.
It's up to you.

Did you know that poor communication is the number one reason for the failure of 86 percent of failed marriages? Successful CEOs lead in many ways, but the most successful are always good communicators. Communication is a key to a better life and better relationships. We can all improve our communication skills, but it takes some work and discipline.

I have a yellowed notepad on my desk in my office. In my best handwriting, which is still questionable, it reads, "AWE." Those three letters have significantly changed my communication for the better. They stand for affection, warmth, and encouragement. But before I jump into the explanation, let me nerd out for just a moment. Experts in the field of communication all agree that nonverbal communication is often more powerful than verbal communication. No doubt words are important, but so are our tone of voice, body language, and facial expressions. In truth, my body language or facial expressions have contradicted words I have said to my wife. Experts tell us that people will trust our body language more than our words. This became a wakeup call for me to understand that communication isn't just about words.

I have found that it's my words that mess up my communication more than anything else. One day as I was thinking about the needs of my wife and kids, I wrote down AWE on that notepad and it changed the way I communicate not only with my family but also with my friends, coworkers, and even people I meet at speaking engagements. Obviously, there are various levels of showering someone with AWE. For example, affection can look very different with your spouse or kids than with a boss or an acquaintance. But I believe AWE is the foundation for good communication.

Affection

While affection is important in all communication— word and deed—let's talk about physical affection in your family. Research has shown that it takes eight to ten meaningful touches a day to maintain physical and emotional health. Think about it: that's not happening in even the most vigilant and intentional families. Many people have a deep craving for affection. Some call it skin hunger. Research teaches us that people who don't get their dose of affectionate touch seem less happy, are lonelier, and are more likely to suffer depression.

If you're married, does your spouse feel loved, safe, and secure with your affection? Your kids need affection, but do they get enough of it from you? If you don't shower them with appropriate affection, they may look elsewhere, and it may not be where you want them to look. Parents can help shape a child's happiness for life with the proper doses of affection.

Remember that showering your loved ones with affection is not just about physical touch but also about appreciation and positive connection, both verbal and nonverbal. I love my dad, but because of his upbringing, he didn't really know how to show affection to his four sons. No doubt part of his affection was working hard and providing for his family. I watched him soften in his later years, especially with the grandchildren, but showing affection was never modeled for him, so he didn't pass it on to his children. I had to learn to show appreciation and affection to loved ones.

One man told me that he was raised in a formal, conservative home with little show of affection from his parents. Otherwise they were good people who provided for his well-being. He told me he was having trouble showing affection to his wife and his kids. I said, "I have three words for you: 'Get over it!'" I was only partly kidding, but it's important to consider ways to work on returning to natural expressions of care and compassion. Again, even if touch isn't their love language, giving people, especially your family, the affection they need in whatever form they prefer is vital and worth the effort. You can learn to be more affectionate. It just takes more work for some people.

I'll never forget meeting a high schooler, Julie, who was caught in the act with her boyfriend in her parents' bedroom during school hours one day when her mom came home from work unexpectedly. Julie was totally embarrassed, and her parents were devastated. They came to see me, and although the couch in my office isn't very large, Mom and Dad sat on one side and Julie sat on the other, hugging the end, leaving a big gap in the middle.

The dad told me the story. He was extremely angry and called her some horrible names. Apparently, she had only recently met this boy, and while his wife cried and agreed with him, Julie kept her head down, tears dripping from her chin. The conversation was going nowhere fast, so I asked the parents if I could talk with Julie alone.

Once the parents were gone, knowing she was likely thinking I was going to yell at her too, I said to Julie, "That was rough."

Finally, after an awkward silence, she looked up, and I gave her a half smile.

She said, "I used to be close to my dad." I hadn't asked about her dad. "He's the one who taught me how to play tennis." I learned she was an all-state tennis champion, and that when she was little, she used to sit on his lap when he came home from work and he read books to her. "He would always grab me in his arms and ask, 'How's my little princess?' I guess I'm not his princess anymore because of all the stuff I do." Her eyes filled with tears again, and I saw such deep pain in them.

I asked if I could bring her parents back in, and as they entered, the mood had changed. Julie was looking at me, and the parents sat a bit closer and held hands.

"How's your relationship with your daughter?" I asked the dad.

He looked at her and then back at me. "We used to be close. I'm the one who taught her to play tennis. I used to read to her and wrestle with her when she was little." Then he got a more serious tone. "Jim, one of the highpoints of my life was coming home from work and Julie running up to me. I'd lift her to the sky and say, 'How's my little princess?'" His eyes filled with tears. "We've had a tough few years, and I've backed off a bit."

I looked at him and then at his wife and said, "My friend, if you don't shower Julie with loads of appropriate affection, there are plenty of guys who would love to offer her a false kind of affection and more."

All humans need meaningful touch to thrive, but affection is also communicated through a smile or an act of kindness. Everyone struggles some with this, so we all need to learn to speak and show appreciation and appropriate care to the people in our lives. Affection at home is different than at the office or in public. But healthy affection signals safety and trust. It's one of the strongest positive connectors and provides one of our finest ways to communicate.

Warmth

Warmth in our communication is all about the atmosphere and tone of our relationships. Warmth is less about the words and more about the positive and inviting environment we present. Honestly, when it comes to good communication, some people are tone deaf.

I believe one person has the power to change the atmosphere in a relationship. My mom was that kind of a person. I grew up in a family of all boys, alcoholism was prevalent, and sometimes the tension was felt more than it was discussed. Mom was the kind of person who could tell it like it is, but at the same time, she created an atmosphere of warmth in our home.

When I was a teenager, my friends often stopped by my house to see if I was home. She would tell whoever it was that I was down at the school gym playing basketball. Typically, whatever friend had stopped by would then say, "Mrs. Burns, can I come in and just hang out with you?" No doubt that friend was welcomed into the house and given some awesome dessert that she just happened to have made that day. My kids called her "the party-time grandma." Mom had the ability to make you feel special. She treated most anyone she came into contact with as an honored guest. That's creating warmth.

At her funeral, person after person got up to share her incredible impact on their lives. For the most part, they all said the same thing, that she treated them with respect and brought warmth, joy, and acceptance into their lives. How's the communication of warmth in your life? What will people say about you at your funeral? When it's cold, we are always drawn to warmth.

It can be difficult to create warmth, but don't forget that homes and relationships with a critical environment are always more susceptible to deception than homes where there is a lot of grace and affirmation. Nagging, negativity, and constant criticism, even if it's a bit justified, shut down intimacy and connection. As my friend Doug Fields likes to say, "You are almost always better off not saying everything you think." My mom taught me the secret was not necessarily to avoid conflict but to choose your battles and hold your tongue when it's just not that important.

Encouragement

A home filled with tension, criticism, and negativity not only shuts down communication and connection but also closes a person's spirit. To encourage and uplift the family, you need a home filled with affirmation and encouragement, which opens up a spirit and paves the way for deeper communication. To move someone from discouraged to encouraged is a great skill, and one to aspire to acquiring.

Philosopher William James once said, "The deepest principle in human nature is the craving to be appreciated." And Mark Twain said, "I can live two months on one good compliment." I think they both are right. Far too many people spend too much of their time in negative communication thinking that it will change a relationship for the better, when lots of encouragement is what is proven to be the most powerful force for transformation. It's harder for people who grew up underappreciated or underencouraged. If you were raised in a home where your parents' style of child-rearing was shame based, then your tendency will be to communicate the same way. Like many people, you'll have to work a bit harder to unlearn bad habits from your past and relearn a better way. But it's all the more important and ultimately rewarding when you do.

Jesus modeled the way to encourage someone when he called out a fisherman who was far from perfect. His name was Simon, but Jesus gave him the nickname Peter. Peter, which means "rock" or "stone" in Greek, had no idea what a gift his new name would be for him. Simon Peter became the rock and leader of the early church because Jesus believed in him. Jesus even exclaimed, perhaps as a pun with a double meaning, "And upon this rock [Peter], I will build my church." Peter lived up to the positive affirmation and ultimately became what Jesus encouraged him to become, despite a few stops and starts along the way.

Are you the greatest cheerleader your spouse has in his or her life? Who is cheering on your kids the most? I hope it's you. At work, is your communication style encouraging or negative? No one said this is easy, because the closer you live or work in proximity, the easier it is to become frustrated with and mad at those people. I have a sign in my office that reads, "Every child needs at least one caring adult who is irrationally positive about them." Communicating encouragement has to do with truly listening to people. Listening, as they say, is the language of love.

Communicating encouragement is showing interest and empathy and seeking to understand. It was Saint Francis of Assisi who prayed, "May I seek to understand rather than to be understood." When it comes down to it, communicating with encouragement is so much more than just saying "good job." It's believing in the person and showering them with appreciation, understanding, and love. This kind of communication is life giving and life changing.

It was a tough time for me when my mom died. Other than Cathy and now my three daughters, Mom was the most important woman in my life. I've never met a person better at communicating AWE than Mom, and she had no training at all in communication. She just figured it out. Eventually, she was moved to hospice with lung cancer. She spent the rest of her shortened life in a hospice bed in her and Dad's bedroom. When I knew she was dying, I didn't want to miss her last days on earth. I could see her moving toward her eternal home, and I was happy for it because her cancer was painful, but I also knew I would miss this incredible woman who encouraged me the most in the world.

I had a dilemma. I was supposed to travel for twenty-four hours to speak to eight thousand students at a conference at Colorado State University. I had booked the engagement a year in advance, and things can always come up, but this was different. It was my mom's last days on earth. I called the organizers of the event and told them what was going on. They were gracious but still hoped I would come. We put off the decision until the day I was supposed to travel. I packed a suitcase but wasn't sure if I was going to fly. It would depend on my mom's health.

Cathy and I drove very early over to my mom and dad's house. She was surprised to see me because she thought I was on my way to Colorado. She had not been doing well, but this day she was sitting up and looked great.

"Jimmy, I thought you were going to Colorado."

I didn't want to say, "Well, Mom, I wasn't sure how you were going to be doing." So I just said, "I'm still thinking about it."

Dad walked into the bedroom. "Look at your mom, she is doing great." He added, "Go to Colorado, Jimmy. We will be right here when you get back tomorrow."

I looked at Cathy and we decided. I would go.

Quickly I said goodbye and began to leave. My mom called me back to her and she cupped my face and kissed me on the forehead. I left in a hurry, still questioning my decision but pressing on. That night, we had a wonderful conference at Colorado State, and then Cathy called me. My mom had died. I was heartbroken that I had not been there.

After a rough night, I boarded the earliest flight I could to get back home. As I sat down in my seat, I asked myself the craziest question: "What were the last words my mother said to me?" In the hustle and bustle of leaving, I had forgotten that when she called me back and kissed my forehead, she said, "Jimmy, I love you, and I'm proud of you."

As I sat there in that seat on the plane, my eyes filled with tears. I realized it was just like Mom to express AWE even in her last words.

I want to be that kind of communicator. Don't you?

SET EXCELLENT GOALS AND CREATE WORKABLE HABITS

*Habits are the compound
interest of self-improvement.*

—JAMES CLEAR

My father was raised on a farm in Kansas that had some cattle. He often told the story of how the cattle regularly got lost because they kept their heads down to eat the grass. They would move from one patch of grass to another, eventually veering off the property and becoming disoriented. Maybe that's why we don't see cows in the circus—they're not real smart.

This is a perfect picture of what can happen to a well-intentioned life if we don't look ahead and set excellent goals, and then create workable habits to attain those goals.

Goals can keep you from drifting. Too many people are like those cows. They are so busy and distracted just trying to make it through the day. Periodically, they glance up only to notice that they have been drifting off course.

I had the rare opportunity to meet an astronaut. He was such an incredible person, and talk about someone with amazing goals and habits! I asked him what it was like being so far from home with someone else on earth partially controlling his destiny. He said, "I trust the plan. And even though we thoroughly go over every aspect of the flight plan, we are constantly making course corrections, or we would drift away." Maybe the difference between a cow and an astronaut is that while they both have goals, one doesn't make course corrections and the other does. Maybe this is a strange illustration, but I think you get the point. In certain aspects of my life, I think I've been more like a cow than an astronaut.

When you write out your goals (and share them with someone else), you are writing out a script or life plan. It's much easier to aim at something if you know what and where the target is. People in business often write out their goals and measure their business success by them. But how about goals for your relationships, spiritual life, and physical health? Even some of the best goal setters for sales and business don't apply to their personal lives the same principles with the same amount of energy, and then they wonder why they are failing in some of their primary relationships and personal goals. It's possible to achieve high goals in business and work but live without any such intention in the other areas of our lives.

I encourage you to write a script for your life that ensures you don't drift. To do this, you'll need to set some realistic goals as a significant part of your life plan. Goals help you get where you want to go. They provide direction and give hope for the future. So think of them accordingly.

What Are Your Goals?

Do you have goals for your personal life and relationships? Have you articulated them? Defining even general, big-picture goals (for example, "I want to have a great marriage") can be an important place to begin. Later you can move toward more specific goals. For example, here is what one couple wrote:

- Go on a weekly date without the kids.
- Learn something new together, like photography or dancing.
- Pray together five times a week.
- Join a couples' group.
- Create a budget and meet regularly to go over it.

Reaching your goals requires determination. Most people who have achieved great things in their lives have had as many failures as successes (if not more). Successful people set goals because they know the importance of having clear direction. How you spend your time and what you choose as goals will guide your priorities, and your priorities will play a significant role in the success of your life, marriage, and relationships.

I didn't make up this SMART acronym, but over the years it has been very helpful for me as I develop the script for my life. Remember, you can't create goals for someone else, only for yourself. Consider these five attributes of effective goal setting as you think through your goals:

1. *Specific.* Are my goals super clear?
2. *Measurable.* How will I track my progress?
3. *Attainable.* What primary obstacles could keep me from reaching my goals, and how will I know when I have attained them?

4. *Relevant.* Why is this goal important to me, and what impact will it have on my life, marriage, work, and children?
5. *Time bound.* What is the date by which I hope to accomplish my goal?

Once you have finished reading this life lesson, consider recording a few SMART goals. Keep them somewhere close to you and go over them regularly. I used to say this phrase to my kids when they were growing up: "He or she who aims at nothing gets there every time!" If it has been awhile since you have set healthy goals, perhaps this lesson can serve as a gentle reminder. (Note: you can take a peek at my own goals in the appendix.)

Create Workable Habits

If you have written down your goals and are feeling pretty good about that, great. You are partway there. Now comes creating the workable plan to reach them.

If you're anything like me, you're an expert at setting great goals and then not reaching them. At the beginning of each new year, each of us in my support group shares our goals. For more than ten years, I kept the same goal to lose fifteen pounds. A few years back when we reviewed our goals at the end of the year, one of the guys asked me how I did with my weight loss goal. I sheepishly admitted I had gained three more pounds. What was missing for me was a plan to follow through on my good intentions.

I finally lost those fifteen pounds when I created a workable plan to help me measure my progress and know when I was drifting. It started by choosing the pain of discipline over the pain of regret and by creating workable habits. What helped me greatly was to follow what I call the one percent rule.

Small Changes Produce Amazing Outcomes

The one percent rule is all about making small changes that will eventually produce amazing outcomes. This concept works in business, relationships, and personal life. James Clear in his excellent book *Atomic Habits* explains that it's often not the big changes that make a difference; rather, it's the tiny ones that create healthy habits over the long haul. He describes it this way: "Improving by one percent isn't notable—sometimes it isn't even noticeable—but it can be far more meaningful, especially in the long run. Here's how the math works out: if you can get one percent better each day for a year, you will end up thirty-seven times better by the time you are done."[16] Unfortunately, the same is true if we get one percent worse each day.

I brought up onstage at a marriage conference a couple who told me they had been happily married for more than sixty years. Both were using walkers as they joined me. I asked them for the secret to the success of their marriage. I loved their answer, and it fits perfectly with the one percent rule. "We said on our wedding day we would show love, grace, kindness, forgiveness, and affection today," the husband said. "And then repeat the process day after day for the next sixty years." The audience applauded, and this lovely couple gave each other one of the most passionate kisses I had seen in a long time. It almost made me blush. Someone yelled, "Get a room!" Everyone laughed, and the husband just smiled, gave a thumbs up, and said, "Later, dude!"

My guess is the secret to their marital success wasn't just their physical attraction toward each other more than sixty years ago, because physical sparks often fade. Rather, it was their daily acts of love toward each other. Practice makes perfect, and growth takes patience and perseverance. The one percent rule teaches us, "You get what you repeat." It's the small changes you make that produce the best outcomes.

My friend Janet is one of the finest people I know. She would be the first to tell you that she is an alcoholic. But she is a recovering alcoholic who has chosen sobriety, because she knows if she doesn't work her plan daily, she could return to a dependency to help her cope with stress.

For years, she tried being sober on her own and failed miserably. Janet would also tell you that she is one of the most fortunate people alive because her husband and kids stayed with her through some awful times. Like many, after hitting bottom several times, she found herself desperate.

Her husband and kids finally said, "You enter treatment and become sober or we are leaving you for good." Her sixth visit to a treatment center, she wrote this one goal: "I will remain sober for the rest of my life." She added, "I'll do it one day at a time." She developed a sobriety plan of discipline, accountability, perseverance, and dropping old habits while building healthy new ones. She began to practice the one percent rule every day. Each week, each month, she learned to bring success in every area of her life. Janet went back to school and eventually received a PhD in chemical dependency. The turnaround is remarkable. She is making a difference in the lives of others, and it all started with a goal and a workable plan. She would tell you it's worth it.

I know so many powerful stories, as I'm sure you do too, of people, heroes really, who have done great things by applying the one percent rule. One of the most inspirational friends in my life is Rod Emery, a guy whom I have the privilege of spending most

Tuesday mornings with. Almost twenty years ago, Rod had a major stroke. To look at him today, you would never know it. He was taken to the hospital, unable to move or speak. He told me that he wondered whether he was going to die. As he was in the ambulance on the way to the hospital, he made a mental checklist of his relationship with God and his relationship with his wonderful wife, Pam, and his two sons. He thought about who would take care of his thriving real estate business. He decided if he was going to die, he was ready, but at the same time he breathed a prayer to God about coming out of the dilemma a better man. His brain was fuzzy, but once at the hospital emergency room, he realized his goal was to have a full recovery.

The problem was he was paralyzed from his neck down, he couldn't talk, and his memory was gone. Eventually, he figured out how to ask the nurse to remove his socks. She reluctantly agreed, and he spent the entire day focused on moving just one toe, and then one finger. By the end of the first day, he had achieved a small victory, and it was progress.

The doctor and the occupational therapist wanted to talk to him about his new normal, but the next day he moved more toes and more fingers. The medical team did not know what to do when he got up to walk. He was wobbly and needed help, but his goal was to walk around the nurses' station, and eventually he was doing laps. Later he got in trouble for walking up and down the stairs.

His recovery was not supposed to happen, let alone so quickly or completely. But the one percent rule worked to get his body and memory back. With the help of his wife and his business assistant, he relearned his business and everything about his family, and day by day he gradually improved. The medical world called it a miracle, but it was fueled by his deep desire to create a workable plan and follow it to achieve goals for the rest of his life.

Today, Rod is active in every way and leads one of the most successful real estate businesses in Orange County. He helps create life change daily through his philanthropy and acts of generosity. And it never would have happened if he hadn't decided to do the hard work of setting a goal to recover and creating a workable plan to do it.

If so many people like Rod and Janet can achieve impossible things with goals and the habits to reach them, why not you and me?

DELEGATE TO FOCUS ON WHAT YOU DO WELL

Do what you were created to be,
and you will set the world on fire.

—CATHERINE OF SIENA

Hi, my name is Jim, and I'm a people-pleaser.

If there were a People-Pleasers Anonymous, I probably could be the president. I think I've been a people-pleaser all my life. It comes naturally. I like to make people happy, and I never want to disappoint anyone at any time. I'm a helper (number 2 on the Enneagram, if that means anything to you). You want a helper around you because they often bring great empathy and compassion to situations. Helpers are feelers. We are usually intuitive, and we certainly want to please you, sometimes at the cost of our healthiness.

Until recent years, I didn't realize that being a people-pleaser, which often has brought great joy and affirmation, also has been toxic to my personal life, leadership, health, and some of my primary relationships. People-pleasers who are good at it, like I am, are usually too busy and end up juggling like crazy. We can easily move toward burnout because we have never learned the lesson of this chapter: delegate. If there is one life lesson I wish I had learned earlier in life, this is it. I've often wondered whether my people-pleasing was a factor in my coming down with cancer. Just today I tweeted, "When you fail, don't fail to miss the lesson." I got a huge response on social media. I'm guessing others need that reminder too.

This lesson has to do with Cathy's frequent statement to me that we already have a messiah and I don't need to replace him. As I've mentioned, I have found that as a husband, as a father, and particularly as a leader, I often take on more than I can accomplish. And while I'm talking about my flaws, I also can put too much effort into areas of my work that I shouldn't be doing.

If you ever feel this way, know that you are in good company. Moses had the same problem, as the story about a visit from his father-in-law, Jethro, shows.

Jethro was a priest of Midian and the father of Zipporah, Moses' wife. (I've always wondered what Moses nicknamed her. Zip? Zippi? Zipper? I don't know, maybe they didn't have nicknames in those days.) Jethro came to visit with Moses to see what God was doing with the people of Israel. (See Exodus 18.) The first day, Jethro and Moses had dinner together, and the very next day, Moses was back at work serving as judge for the people "from morning till evening."

Moses was overcommitted.

Jethro asked his son-in-law a good question: "Why do you alone sit as judge . . . from morning till evening?"

He continued, "What you are doing is not good. You and these people who come to you will only wear yourselves out. The work is too heavy for you; you cannot handle it alone."

Jethro gave Moses a plan to delegate some of his work to others. The plan was a good one. He basically suggested that Moses get out of the being-the-judge-for-everyone business and delegate that work to other capable people. And that is exactly what he did.

I love the quote at the start of this chapter: "Do what you were created to be, and you will set the world on fire." To live the way Catherine of Siena suggests is to figure out how to delegate responsibilities so you can focus on what you do best. The most effective people I know are willing to delegate to others in order to get more done in their own gifting. First you must ask yourself, "What am I gifted to do?" For some people, that alone can take a while. But ask around if you need help. Then, a good question to consider is, "If I had no choice but to give 75 percent of my work to somebody, what would I delegate?" This exercise can be enormously clarifying.

At the same time, realize that delegating work, though it might not seem evident, helps others too. People are made to help each other and to be given tasks that help them define who they are. Delegating works wonders in teaching others and equipping our children as well.

Often, delegating is a simple matter of understanding what needs to happen to shift responsibility, and the steps for training others to take on the responsibilities we once had are straightforward. Whether it's in our jobs or in the training of our children, the process is called the Four Phases of Ease.[17]

- *Phase 1: I do it, you watch.* I do the work, but you watch how I do it in preparation for learning how to do it yourself.
- *Phase 2: I do it, you do it.* Now we do the work together. I give insight and wisdom from my experience, but now we are a team.
- *Phase 3: You do it, I assist.* Now you are in charge, but I am still there to help when needed.

- *Phase 4: You do it.* Now you do it, and I either find something else to do or, better yet, do something I love to do and do it well.

Here are three questions to ask yourself about your workload:

1. Do I feel overloaded much or most of the time?
2. Is there something I'm doing right now that someone else can do or learn to do?
3. Do I put enough of my attention on things I am gifted for?

To be a more effective delegator and answer those three questions in a healthy manner, you must learn how to say no and become ruthless about your priorities.

As I was going through a reorganization of my mind and life goals, I wrote down two words in my journal: ruthless prioritization. For anyone like me who tends to use busyness to earn "pleaser" points, ruthless prioritization means saying no to good things and good opportunities in order to say yes to the most important priorities. As I ranked my priorities and reevaluated my schedule and focus, I realized that a lot of things screaming for my attention were not my top priorities. I had to learn to say no.

I remember speaking at a Promise Keepers pastors' conference many years ago at the Arizona

127

Diamondbacks' Bank One Ballpark. The band was playing, and I was backstage getting ready to speak. I was sitting next to a dear man named Jack Hayford, who was the emcee for the event. Jack had been a mentor of mine over the years and a person I considered to be one of the great leaders of his generation. I asked him, "Jack, what is the secret to your leadership success all these years?"

He thought about it for a moment and then said, "Jim, it's not about the things I have chosen to do as much as the things I have chosen not to do. I've had to say no to some great opportunities to say yes to the most important. I have needed to be ruthless about my priorities."

That solidified it for me.

As I looked into the lives of people like Jack who not only were incredible leaders but had strong family relationships, I realized they had developed the discipline to move from overwhelming multitasking to being single-focus, task-oriented people. It hit me one day when I was feeling especially overwhelmed. My to-do list was eight pages long, and no one and nothing was getting my full attention. In relationships and projects, I was economizing and skimming time from almost all areas of my life. It's hard to be efficient and effective when you are too busy. I knew I needed to move from economizing and skimming to eliminating and concentrating on the most important things. Then I saw a simple diagram that was a great reminder of what I needed to do: I call it "The Success Diagram."

The Success Diagram

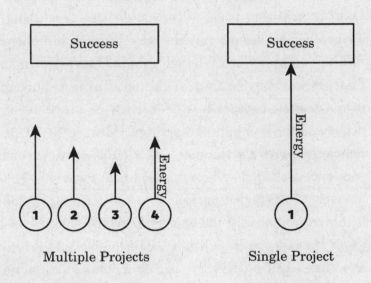

Multiple Projects   Single Project

Let me summarize this with an old Russian proverb: "If you chase two rabbits, you will not catch either one." In trying to please everyone and taking on too many projects, my performance was mediocre in everything, including my relationships. For me, multitasking equals average results, feeling disappointed in myself, knowing I can do better but not having the emotional or physical energy to do my best. I also knew that when I did have a singular focus on something, the results were amazing. I found single-tasking to be better in most ways, but it takes a lot of discipline and focus as well as the breaking of some old habits. You must learn to:

Do the one thing. The key to getting off the multi-tasking train is pretty simple: do the one thing. Typically, you know what the one thing is, but there are just so many other lesser things that sometimes distract us from getting to the one thing.[18] This is not a new concept. It has been with us since Jesus declared, "Live one day at a time" (Matt. 6:34 TLB). Sobriety comes one moment at a time. Henry Ford was once asked how he created an automobile. His answer: "Nothing is particularly hard if you divide it into small jobs." And I'm certain you've heard this joke: "How do you eat a whale?" The answer: "One bite at a time." But practically speaking, what can you do to accomplish this?

Limit distractions. Perhaps one of the biggest obstacles to a better focus are the distractions we allow into our lives. Technology is undoubtedly the biggest of those distractions. It has blurred the boundaries in our lives. Text messages, on average, are answered within thirty seconds. Facebook, Instagram, Twitter, TikTok, YouTube, Snapchat, email, and all the other social media apps on our phone steal hours a day from most people. Do we really need to be as connected as we are, twenty-four hours a day, seven days a week? There is only one healthy answer to that question: no!

To become more focused, we need longer periods of uninterrupted time. Learning to live much of our day in "airplane mode" is a great discipline. It takes an average of twenty-three minutes and fifteen seconds to get back to a task after an interruption.[19] Except for parents of babies and toddlers who need to be present at all times, we need to better manage our interruptions in order to have the time to do what we do best and do what we love.

Make your top priority your top priority. A life-changer for me was a meeting I had with two of my dearest friends, Todd and Doug, some years ago. They asked me what percentage of my time I spent on my top priorities, and what percentage I spent on other important things. Together we figured it was about 50/50. The look on their faces said it all. "You need to ruthlessly prioritize and do that one right thing. Start doing what you love a lot more, and do it well." It was easy for me to come up with my core eight priorities. (See diagram "Core Eight Priorities.") What was much more difficult was to cut priorities that were getting in the way of my core eight. I also had to think about how much time to invest in those eight priorities. It's not a simple exercise, and there are no magic numbers, but it's good to designate an amount of time you intend to spend each week on your priorities.

Core Eight Priorities

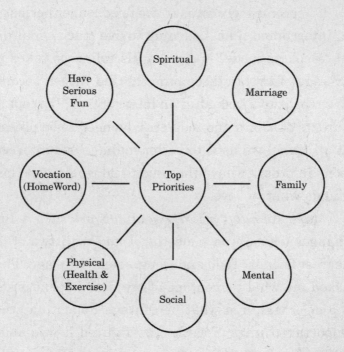

Now answer these questions:

- Am I giving enough attention to the most important priorities in my life?
- What is the one thing that would benefit me most in each area?

Many people I talk to tell me that they often feel overwhelmed, unfocused, and weary from the life they have chosen. If you feel that way, you don't have to continue down that same path. There is another way toward doing what you love and doing it well. You may just need to say no and to delegate to get there.

Life is short. Don't let it slip by focused on a to-do list that doesn't express or squelches your heart.

I always think of the classic movie *Chariots of Fire*, when Eric Liddell makes the memorable statement, "I believe that God made me for a purpose, for China. But he also made me fast. And when I run, I feel his pleasure." God has given you gifts and abilities, purpose and meaning. You were designed to make a difference. What are you doing or not doing to foster your special gifts from God?

GLORIFY AND ENJOY GOD WHILE SERVING HIM FOREVER

I have one desire now—to live a life of reckless abandon for the Lord, putting all my energy and strength into it.

—ELISABETH ELLIOT

Alex Trebek died on November 8, 2020. Alex Trebek was a household name in my family. My parents watched the television show *Jeopardy!* from the time it began in 1964 until the time my father died at age eighty-nine in 2008. Alex Trebek became the host of *Jeopardy!* in 1984. *Jeopardy!* even became a part of my honeymoon. Let me explain. There was a *Jeopardy!* board game at the home where we stayed for our honeymoon in Lake Tahoe, California, and Cathy beat me at it fourteen times in a row. Sounds like a pretty romantic honeymoon, doesn't it?

Alex and his amazing wife, Jean, were on a trip to the Holy Land when he started feeling sick. After they returned from a "walking in the footsteps of Jesus" tour in Israel, they were told he had pancreatic cancer. As you know, this is not the kind of cancer you want to get. The recovery rate is very poor. Yet even as Alex went through the toughest of chemo treatments, his wife, Jean, wrote, "With each passing day, I have found so much to be grateful for. Alex's work. Our kids, our friends, a sunset, a flower blooming in our garden. This didn't have to be a death sentence. It could be a life sentence. A constant reminder of how precious life is. The smallest things that I once took for granted now carry more meaning. I think that is how God keeps us in the moment. He focuses us with grace." She went on to describe their new normal, in which they sit on their backyard swing together, feeling the warmth of the sunshine and gazing up at the sky, "knowing we are loved. Not just by each other but by a God who will see us through all things."[20]

Facing death has a way of setting us free from the things that encumber us, focusing us on what's most important and most precious. Cancer caused me to look my mortality straight in the face. It brought clarity to my life in a way nothing else had ever done. Few people like to talk about the inevitable fact that they will die, but it helped me realize there is nothing more important than a right relationship with God and with my loved ones. Anne Lamott put it better than I could ever express it: "My deepest belief is that to live as if we're dying can set us free. Dying people teach you to pay attention and to forgive and not to sweat the small things."[21]

After my diagnosis, things that mattered a lot before cancer just didn't matter as much. And things that hadn't mattered as much before cancer became front and center. As death became more real to me, even though it wasn't necessarily imminent, I kept thinking about the Westminster Confession of Faith. I'd studied this rule of faith and life in my Princeton graduate-school days, but to be honest, I could remember only the first statement and had never fully understood it. Written as a creed in 1646, it asks the question, "What is the chief end of humankind?" From an eternal perspective, is there a more important question? I don't think so. The answer: "To glorify God, and to enjoy him forever." Simple, profound, challenging, beautiful. Do you need to endure cancer or have death knocking on your door to live by this? I don't think so.

For me, this last lesson has become the most

important lesson. Glorify and enjoy God while serving him forever. It has become my mantra, my top priority, what gives me meaning and purpose. It reminds me to tell my family I love them more, to stop and speak to a stranger, or to sit quietly waiting to view the spectacular sunset over the Pacific Ocean I watched last night. Some of the small stuff has become the main stuff. I write this lesson on the first page every time I start a new journal. I add, "Make the most of today while breathing in God's grace." I've also begun adding the beautiful and simple phrase I heard my friend John Ortberg say: "Love God and do the right thing."

I think understanding and living out a grace-based life is where we learn to glorify, enjoy, and serve God. Grace reminds us that it's not about us but about God's unfailing love and mercy. Who has seen you at your very worst? Who have you treated unkindly? Have you ever fought anyone? I have. Yelled at someone? I have. Have you ever lied to or ignored anybody? Ever broken promises? Disappointed anyone? Even been unfaithful? I have. Not to my wife but in my relationship with God. I've done all the above to him and more. Yet God's consistent love, grace, and forgiveness are staggering.

Jesus, our picture of God, said to a woman caught in the act of adultery, "Where are your accusers? Didn't even one of them condemn you?"

"No, Lord," she replied.

He could have condemned her to death. After all, he was God's son. But he said, "Neither do I. Go and sin no more" (John 8:3–11 NLT).

Unmerited favor challenged her to accept God's forgiveness. Such grace causes us all to pause, and it becomes our cause to glorify, enjoy, and serve him.

There is a scene in the Broadway show *Les Miserables*[22] that gets to me every time. I've seen the play at least ten times, and this scene usually brings tears to my eyes. A man, Jean Valjean, has been in prison for nineteen years for stealing a piece of bread for his hungry family. He is finally set free from prison, but not set free from his bitterness. He meets a Catholic bishop. The bishop invites him for a meal unlike anything he has tasted in nineteen years or perhaps even in his entire life. The bishop asks him to stay, but in the middle of the night Valjean slips out of bed and steals most of the silver in the bishop's home. In the morning, he is caught by the authorities and brought back to the bishop with the silver in his bag. But the major twist comes when the good bishop lies to the authorities, telling them he had given Valjean the silver and that he was disappointed Valjean had left the best behind, the silver candlesticks, worth a lot of money. The authorities release him, and Valjean, utterly bewildered, takes the candlesticks from the bishop, receiving his graceful benediction: "Remember this, my brother—see in this some higher plan. . . . Don't forget. Don't ever forget that you promised to become a new man. I bought your soul. And now I give you back to God."

That day, Jean Valjean experiences the love, grace, and forgiveness of God. He spends the rest of his life living a very different story. With the grace given, he freely gives sacrificially to those in need.

Grace is always God driven. I love what my friend Max Lucado once said: "Where the grace of God is missed, bitterness is born. But where the grace of God is embraced, forgiveness flourishes. The longer we walk in the garden, the more likely we are to smell like flowers."[23] For anyone who has experienced deep grace, isn't it natural to want to be a person who bestows grace to others simply to enjoy more grace? People who hold on to bitterness and resentment for too long, even when they have been deeply wounded or wronged, become ugly on the inside. "You only have to forgive once. To resent, you have to do it all day, every day."[24] That's a line from a novel, but just focus on it for a moment. People who hold on to bitterness and resentment have a hard time enjoying God's forgiveness and grace. When someone understands the grace and forgiveness of God, and especially when they receive that kind of love from another, they experience a glimpse of the deepest nature of God himself.

I believe this is the greatest lesson we can learn

from death. And if we could learn to talk about death and think about it more, there are certain facts we could benefit from:

1. We all will die.
2. Life is short, so we should make the most of each day.
3. Celebrate life daily. Live now, don't wait.
4. Walk with and enjoy God, the creator and sustainer of life.

Here is what I have learned from facing my own mortality:

Facing our inevitable death, no matter our age, quality of health, or place in life, teaches us that the time is now to live like we're dying. Don't wait. The time is now to live to the fullest, to put energy into all that is good. When we face tough issues, we shouldn't face them alone. Facing our mortality reminds us to lean into a right relationship with God and a right relationship with our loved ones. It puts our priorities in the right place. Now is the time to:

• Pick up the phone and call a person you love.
• Live today and every day celebrating moments. Take joy in small moments and find the beauty in them.
• Delight in the accumulation of these days,

one after another. It's your life; it's always up to you.

- Watch more sunsets and take in the beauty of creation every day.
- Make sure you have at least one friend who is about four years old to make you smile.
- Put aside unnecessary worry, because worry is useless and will paralyze your joy.
- Attack problems with grace, but only real ones and not imaginary ones.
- Drop all grudges, bitterness, and resentment.
- Hug a special person in your life today. Tell them you love them and are proud of them.

Now is also the time to invest in what has eternal value, the miraculous in the mundane, the people behind the interruptions and distractions, the deeper meaning within the daily. Don't neglect spending more moments with God or drift from his love or forfeit your spiritual purpose. Let go of "more" to lean into the eternal. Don't put off Bible study or forget to pray. Find that job you love and really live in that home (the one you can afford). Take care of feeding your soul, not your things or your house. Don't miss out on a meaningful relationship because you couldn't see beyond the task at hand.

Death teaches us, if we are willing to hear it, that the time is now. Jesus said it perfectly: "Don't be anxious about tomorrow. God will take care of your tomorrow too. Live one day at a time" (Matt. 6:34 TLB). I'm convinced the way to do this best is to breathe in God's grace and then give it to someone else.

Start living with that eternal perspective today.

APPENDIX

It is often helpful to look at others' goals and workable habits. Here is a shortened version of my goals that I shared with my support group and my wife. I try to incorporate the SMART plan for goals as well as making sure the goals have a workable system that become habits. It's always a work in process!

2020 Goals (with systems where needed)

Personal, Marriage, and Family

1. Put time and energy into my relationship with Cathy
   a. Weekly spiritual time
   b. Prayer daily
   c. Date weekly (add to the calendar)
   d. Continued work on financial planning (financial plan done by June 30)

  e. Enjoy more time together away (create
   together and put on the calendar)

  f. Extended times on the calendar. We do
   better away.

2. Work on my physical plan (personal training is
 the system)

  a. Goal: fifteen more pounds

  b. 70,000 steps a week

  c. Three times a week in the gym

  d. Stretching most every day

  e. Stay mainly off sugar, little "whites,"
   stricter on calories

  f. Accountable on a monthly basis

3. Family

  a. Put energy and regular time into the lives
   of my sons-in-law

  b. Annual family get-together in July

  c. Be supportive, showing leadership, and
   speak into their lives when invited

  d. Keep up our commitments with James and
   Charlotte

Spiritual Growth

1. Continue daily with the One Year Bible, *Jesus
 Calling*, and journal

2. Tuesday morning group

3. More extended time with God on a regular
 basis (put dates on calendar with the plan)

4. More rest and more margin (add to the calendar and have group hold accountable)
5. Take more days off (add to the calendar for the next six months)
6. Read six spiritual growth books this year (create the list of books to read and get started by January 1)
7. Listen to a weekly message podcast by the best of communicators (add to calendar and be held accountable)

HomeWord

1. Continue to create the "new and improved" HomeWord
   a. Ministry model, finances, leadership
   b. What do the next fifteen years look like? Partnerships, younger and fresh leadership
   c. Meet with board chair monthly to review plan
2. Finish *Have Serious Fun* book by August 1. Film the course by September 15.
3. Develop *The Marriage Course* by end of year
4. Create HomeWord Digital. Add digital component to seminars and Trainer of Trainers by October 1.

QUESTIONS FOR PERSONAL REFLECTION OR GROUP DISCUSSION

Preface

1. Sometimes significant experiences can wake us up or even force us into seasons of great change. For Jim, learning he had cancer was a catalyst. What experience or experiences have caused you to make a profound change in your life?

2. There are many great quotes in this book. Jim says that this one from C. S. Lewis summarizes his theme: "You can't go back and change the beginning, but you can start where you are and

change the ending." How does this quote apply to
your life and thinking?

3. If you were making a list of key lessons or phrases
that you have learned in your life, what would
they be?

4. Have you taken the time to think about your
legacy? What words describe how you want to be
remembered?

5. What are some things you hope to take away from
reading this book?

Lesson 1: Have Serious Fun

1. How is the fun factor in your life? On a scale of 1 to 10, how often do you feel the seriousness of life weighing you down?

2. Despite the serious and negative circumstances in your life, do you still make time to have fun? How so?

3. "A cheerful heart is good medicine, but a broken spirit saps a person's strength" (Prov. 17:22 NLT). How have you seen this proverb working in your life?

4. Play builds great memories. What memories do you have of fun that helped you connect with someone or improved your life?

5. Play reduces stress. Jim wrote five questions to know whether you are overstressed. How did you do with those questions? Are you overstressed?

Lesson 2: Attitude Is Everything

1. Henry Cloud told Jim that you can't just choose joy but rather you need to "choose the practices and activities that enrich your life with joy." How have you seen that work in your life? And are there new practices or activities you might incorporate to enrich your life with joy?

2. According to the Pie Chart of Happiness, only 10 percent of our joy comes from circumstances. Does this finding surprise you? Are you leaning in to enough healthy activities to help bring you more happiness?

3. How do prayer and spiritual practices help with your happiness mindset?

4. Your circumstance may never change, but your attitude can change, and that makes all the difference in the world. Think of a time when that principle has worked in your life.

5. Joni Eareckson Tada told Jim that giving thanks in all circumstances had become her "reflex reaction." How does this principle help your attitude?

Lesson 3: Practice Thank Therapy

1. Thank therapy is a process of daily acknowledging God's gift of life and naming reasons to be thankful. Name five reasons why you are thankful.

2. Think of a tough situation in your life right now. What are a few reasons to be thankful even in this tough situation?

3. Science reveals that thankfulness can unshackle us from toxic emotions and even have lasting positive effects on our brains. Think of a time when you experienced something like this.

4. John Ortberg says that a mindset of gratitude "liberates us from the prison of self-preoccupation." Think of the most fulfilled person you know. Do they have a mindset of thankfulness? What might you do to be more like this person?

5. God tends to do his greatest work through people who have grateful, trusting hearts. Thankfulness opens the door to God's presence. When have you deeply felt God's presence? Was thankfulness a factor in that experience?

Lesson 4: If the Devil Can't Make
You Bad, He'll Make You Busy

1. "Perhaps one of the greatest problems in this world is the breathless pace at which we live our lives." Do you agree with this statement? Why or why not?

2. Busyness and hurry are a "form of violence on the soul." How do you see this principle playing out in your life and the lives of those around you?

3. Constant busyness and fatigue cause health and relationship problems. What have you done in your life to cure the hurry sickness syndrome?

4. Are you overloaded? How did you do with the ten questions Jim asked about the overload syndrome? What one or two decisions could you make to improve?

5. Which of these sabbath prescriptions do you most want to work on: rest, refresh, restore, or recreate? Does anything come to mind that you can do this week to make a small but important change?

Lesson 5: Practice Positive Adaptability

1. Would you say that you are an adaptable person, or is adaptability an area that needs improvement?

2. Asking "does it really matter?" is a principle that Jim says provides great benefits to any relationship. What do you think makes this principle important? What makes it difficult to accomplish?

3. Jim says, "Positivity is the twin of adaptability." How might these characteristics be related? Do you practice "learned optimism"?

4. Negativity can devour happiness in a relationship. Where do you see negativity hurting a relationship in your life?

5. What advice would you give to an "awfulizer"—someone who always imagines the worst?

Lesson 6: It's the Pain of Discipline or the Pain of Regret

1. How have you recently experienced the pain of regret encouraging you to accept the pain of discipline?

2. How often do busyness and a hurried pace in your life cause this principle to fail?

3. Jim writes about "a day in the life of Jesus," which he began with solitude, then moved to community

with his replenishing relationships, and then to his work. How does this structure compare with your typical day? What's different?

4. Grit is a great word when it comes to discipline. In what areas of your life could you use a large dose of grit to get things under control or moving forward?

5. To persevere in life, you need grit and discipline. Can you think of someone you know who applied perseverance and it paid off? How did they do it?

Lesson 7: Family Matters More Than Work

1. Why do you think a lot of people struggle with prioritizing their work ahead of their families?

2. Have you experienced what Jim calls "confused priorities"? What were they for you?

3. Many people deal with overcoming negative family patterns. Are there issues from your family's past that still cause you strain? If you have some negative family patterns, what key ones need work?

4. In her research on dying, Elisabeth Kübler-Ross found that people have two dominant desires at the end of their lives: a right relationship with God and a right relationship with their loved ones. How does that understanding help you think about your priorities?

5. Between a person's birth and launching into adulthood there are only 936 weeks. What's one way you might make the most of your family time this week?

Lesson 8: Find Replenishing Relationships

1. Many people report having acquaintances but no deep friendships. Have you ever had a deep friendship? What makes such a relationship so special?

2. Everyone has VDPs (very draining people) and VIPs (very important people) in their lives. Do you have good boundaries with your VDPs? Do you spend enough time with your VIPs—the people who replenish you?

3. Do you have mentors in your life? Who are the people you look to for guidance, coaching, wisdom, and wise counsel?

4. What is one thing of value you have learned from a mentor?

5. There is a proverb that says, "Iron sharpens iron" (Prov. 27:17). How does this proverb encourage you to find and nurture replenishing relationships?

Lesson 9: Seek Accountability for Effectiveness

1. Do you have a "safe place" to be totally honest with someone with whom you share your hurts, worries, pains, joys, hopes, and goals? If you do, you have made a really wise investment. If you don't, what person or group could you build an accountability relationship with?

2. Accountability is security for your life. Jim told a story of a Christian leader who had a moral failure and later it was revealed that he'd had no accountability in his life and neither was he in touch with his "dark side." Have you experienced the vital importance of accountability for keeping you focused on life's top priorities?

3. The Bible says, "Guard your heart above all else, for it determines the course of your life" (Prov. 4:23 NLT). How do you guard your heart in your daily life?

4. There are many obstacles to guarding your heart. Jim mentioned several. Which are the most difficult for you? Are there others you would add?

5. Accountability breeds responsibility. Is there a safe friend you can be brutally honest with? How might you pursue closer accountability with them?

Lesson 10: Communicate with AWE

1. Good communication is a trait commonly found among successful CEOs, and poor communication is the number one reason marriages fail. Who are your models of good communication?

2. AWE is an excellent acronym for communicating with affection, warmth, and encouragement. Which of these is a strength for you? In which would you most like to improve?

3. Was there much affection in your childhood home? How has that influenced your feelings about affection? What would others say about you in the area of affection?

4. How much warmth do you feel in your home? In your workplace? What are you doing to help create an atmosphere of warmth?

5. Philosopher William James once said, "The deepest principle in human nature is the craving to be appreciated." Do the people in your primary relationships feel deeply appreciated by you? Do you feel appreciated by them?

Lesson 11: Set Excellent Goals and Create Workable Habits

1. Without goals, we can't make wise course corrections. How has setting goals worked for you? When has setting a goal not worked for you? Why do you think that happened?

2. When you set goals, do you consider the five attributes that make them SMART: specific, measurable, attainable, relevant, time bound? Write out one fresh goal that has all of these attributes.

3. While setting a goal gets us halfway there, we also need to create workable habits. Describe the habit you will need to reach the goal you thought of in question 2.

4. "Small changes produce amazing outcomes." If over the next year you could improve by 1 percent to

make a major difference in your life, in what area would you improve? Why?

5. Why is living one day at a time so critical to reaching your life-changing goals?

Lesson 12: Delegate to Focus on What You Do Well

1. When Catherine of Siena said, "Do what you were created to be, and you will set the world on fire," she assumed that meant focusing on what is most important and allowing some things to slide. What do you hope to focus on more in the next year? Is there anything you could let slide?

2. How might the "Four Phases of Ease" help in the process of delegating some of your responsibilities? What might you delegate and to whom?

3. Most people find it hard to say no to things that

feel important. How could Jack Hayford's advice to Jim about saying no to some great opportunities in order to say yes to the most important apply to you?

4. Multitasking is critical at times, but success comes from putting all of your energy into one project. How could you rearrange your workday or projects to be more singularly focused?

5. Jim listed his eight core priorities. What are your five to eight core priorities? Answer these two questions: Am I giving enough attention to the most important priorities in my life? What is the one thing that would benefit me most in each area?

Lesson 13: Glorify and Enjoy God While Serving Him Forever

1. What would it mean for you to live a life of reckless abandon for God?

2. John Ortberg's motto is "love God and do the right thing." Do you think living life through this grid could help you make better priorities?

3. Do you agree that it's critical to understand the concept of grace (unmerited favor) in order to glorify and enjoy God? Why or why not?

4. Do you think that if we truly lived what we believe—that life is eternal and life on earth is not—we would be better able to live each day to the fullest? If so, what do you think it would take to live from this perspective more consistently?

5. What does it mean to you to "invest" in the eternal? What one or two changes in your life may help you to live out that principle more effectively over the coming months? Describe what you hope will result from that investment.

NOTES

1. I never thought I was going to die, but my mother-in-law did. She told Cathy, "You and Jim have lived a great life together and you are probably still young enough to find someone else." Gotta love the mother-in-law!
2. Leonard Sweet, *Soul Salsa: Seventeen Surprising Steps for Godly Living in the Twenty-First Century* (Grand Rapids: Zondervan, 2000), 158.
3. Anne Lamott, *Help, Thanks, Wow: The Three Essential Prayers* (New York: Riverhead, 2012), 60–61.
4. The Terry Fox Foundation, "Quotes," https://terryfox.org/terrys-story/quotes/.
5. Joshua Brown and Joel Wong, "How Gratitude Changes You and Your Brain," *Greater Good Magazine*, June 6, 2017, https://greatergood.berkeley.edu/article/item/how_gratitude_changes_you_and_your_brain.
6. Dr. Henry Cloud, Facebook post, August 30, 2016, www.facebook.com/DrHenryCloud/posts/my-work-

and-my-experiences-have-led-me-to-an-abiding-belief-that-grateful-people/10154540798684571/.

7. John Ortberg, *When the Game Is Over, It All Goes Back in the Box* (Grand Rapids: Zondervan, 2007), 149.

8. John Mark Comer, *The Ruthless Elimination of Hurry* (Colorado Springs: Waterbrook, 2019), 47.

9. Richard A. Swenson, *The Overload Syndrome: Learning to Live within Your Limits* (Colorado Springs: NavPress, 1998), 71.

10. Comer, *Ruthless Elimination of Hurry*, 168.

11. Richard Selzer, *Mortal Lessons: Notes on the Art of Surgery* (1987; repr., Orlando: Harcourt Brace, 1996), 45–46.

12. "Awfulize," Lexico.com, https://www.lexico.com/en/definition/awfulize.

13. Angela Lee Duckworth, *Grit: The Power of Passion and Perseverance*, April 2013, www.ted.com/talks/angela_lee_duckworth_grit_the_power_of_passion_and_perseverance#t-136262.

14. Angela Duckworth, *Grit: The Power of Passion and Perseverance* (New York: Scribner, 2018).

15. Brené Brown, *Daring Greatly: How the Courage to Be Vulnerable Transforms the Way We Live, Love, Parent, and Lead* (New York: Avery, 2012), 34.

16. James Clear, *Atomic Habits: An Easy and Proven Way to Build Good Habits and Break Bad Ones* (New York: Random House, 2018), 15.

17. I first learned the Four Phases of Ease from a youth

ministry expert, J. David Stone, in the early 1980s. I have adapted his version here.

18. For an excellent read from more of a business perspective, I recommend *The One Thing: The Surprisingly Simple Truth behind Extraordinary Results* by Gary Keller and Jay Papason (Portland, OR: Bard Press, 2012).

19. Gloria Mark, Daniela Gudith, and Ulrich Klocke, "The Cost of Interrupted Work: More Speed and Stress," n.d., https://www.ics.uci.edu/~gmark/chi08-mark.pdf.

20. Jean Trebek, "Jean Trebek on Finding Joy with Her Husband Alex during Their Greatest Challenge," *Guideposts*, July 27, 2020, https://www.guideposts.org/caregiving/hope-and-inspiration/stories-of-hope-for-caregivers/jean-trebek-on-finding-joy-with-her-husband-alex-despite-his-pancreatic-cancer.

21. Anne Lamott, *Bird by Bird: Some Instructions on Writing and Life* (New York: Anchor, 1994), 117.

22. Claude-Michel Schönberg, *Les Misérables: A Musical* (Milwaukee: Alain Boublil Music, 1998).

23. Max Lucado, *In the Grip of Grace: Your Father Always Caught You. He Still Does* (1996; repr., Nashville: Thomas Nelson, 2014), 136.

24. M. L. Stedman, *The Light between Oceans: A Novel* (New York: Simon and Schuster, 2012), 323.

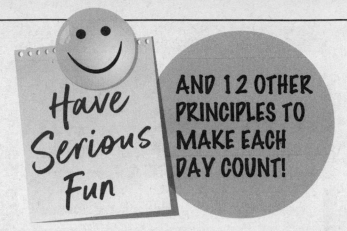

Digital Course for Groups or Individuals

Practical, Proven, Inspirational

Perfect for great discussion and interaction

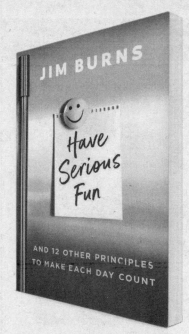

The course includes:

- 7 short videos of inspiring stories from Jim Burns and others
- Great for small groups or individual learning
- One reproducible outline and reflection questions for each video
- One leaders guide

Jim faced mortality with his cancer and was reminded that only a few things are important to make a life worthy. He has shared them here and they are a gift. Thank you, Jim. – Dr. Henry Cloud

For more information go to:

HomeWord.com   (800) 397-9725